INCLUDES **SAMUEL ALITO** ON THE ISSUES

21 SUPREME COURT

ISSUES FACING AMERICA

The Scalia Model for a Conservative Court

Compiled and Edited by STEVE ELLIOTT

WWW.GRASSFIRE.ORG

xulon
PRESS

Acknowledgments

This book is an excellent example of what happens when friends and professional associates come together around a fresh idea and work together to see that idea become reality.

The first spark of this idea was lit nearly two years ago during a dinner conversation with author and book publisher, Tom Freiling. Tom and I discussed something we called "Book Activism" — harnessing the influence of book publishing for conservatism.

On many occasions, Tom and I bounced around different ways to use book activism. Then, one day on the phone, the concept for this book on Antonin Scalia ignited in our minds and we immediately went to work. Tom and I are hopeful that our work here will make a difference in the future of our nation, for our children and for their children.

Special thanks to Bryan T. Mullican for the many hours of research he offered to this project, pouring over the public record and helping to sift through thousands upon thousands of words for those prescient statements from Justice Scalia that best demonstrate his position in each of the topic areas we identified.

Also, thanks to David Shepherd of Broadman & Holman Publishers for his support of this "book activism" strategy.

Finally, the Grassfire.org team once again has stepped forward and enthusiastically supported an untested concept. Randy, Bob, Ron, Chris, Nancy, Julie, Tina, Lisa and the rest of the team – thanks! May our efforts together play even a small role in strengthening our nation's heritage.

Table of Contents

How The Courts Impact Your Life

By Steve Elliott
Founder and president of Grassfire.org

How does the Supreme Court impact the lives of American citizens? Let me count the ways. Twenty-one ways, to be precise.

There is a great political awakening taking place in our nation today as millions of Americans recognize the decisive role the federal courts and specifically the Supreme Court play in our society. Issue after issue seems to come back to some court decision that has imposed a course of action on the nation. This pattern of judicial activism began in the mid 20th Century and became a national issue with the 1973 *Roe v. Wade* decision. Today, judicial activism is not confined to one issue area. From property rights to gun rights to the death penalty to marriage to education, the courts have become the determining factor in the great debates of our day.

Thankfully Americans have awakened to the devastating effects of judicial activism and the tide of history is about to change. A new era of judicial accountability is beginning with a fundamental return to judicial conservatism — the founder's vision of a limited federal court that interprets the Constitution instead of legislating from the bench.

What Americans now know innately — that the Supreme Court has overstepped its bounds and has become our unelected rulers — this book attempts to lay out in a systematic way. *21 Supreme Court*

Issues Facing America offers in a readable format precisely how Supreme Court decisions impact the key debates in our society. But this is not simply a book to point out the problem areas. *21 Supreme Court Issues* focuses on applying a conservative judicial philosophy (what many call an "originalist" philosophy) to the issues of our day and giving citizens a road map for understanding the Supreme Court and the judicial nomination process.

Our research team at Grassfire.org and our partners at Xulon Press have worked together to develop this in-depth resource covering the 21 Supreme Court issues facing America. Grassfire.org is one of the nation's largest and fastest growing conservative citizen organizations, with approximately 1 million active team members nationwide. Xulon Press is an innovative publishing company that is leading a new area of publishing called "book activism" — developing fast-turn books that weigh in on the debates of our day.

This work uses what we call the "Scalia model" to describe a conservative judicial philosophy as applied to the 21 issues. We selected Justice Antonin Scalia because he has become a standard bearer for judicial conservative thought. Not "conservative" in a political sense, rather "conservative" in a judicial sense. Throughout this book the reader will note that Antonin Scalia has resisted the temptation to politicize his judicial role. He has, instead, adhered to a certain view of constitutional interpretation that sets aside personal predilections. Scalia calls himself an "originalist," viewing the Constitution as a statute consisting of words that had an understandable meaning at the time of the adoption of those words. Thus, for Antonin Scalia, the Constitution is not a living document whose meaning changes with the "evolving standards" of society (a meaning ultimately determined by, you guessed it, judges!). To the contrary – the Constitution has a fixed, statutory meaning. A real meaning. Still, Scalia does not call himself a "strict constructionist," preferring to offer that he seeks a "reasonable" interpretation of the Constitution's original meaning.

This perspective defines a conservative judicial philosophy and represents the model whereby readers are encouraged to gain an understanding of the 21 issues and then apply that understanding to nominees such as Samuel Alito.

21 Supreme Court Issues begins here with an examination of the central question at stake: what kind of a Constitution do we have? Is the Constitution a legal document with an understandable, fixed meaning, or is it a living document that should be reinterpreted to adjust to evolving community standards? This debate has far-reaching ramifications in our nation that extend to every aspect of the public debate. This is the first order of business in assessing the current Supreme Court or the nomination of Samuel Alito or any judge or justice. And so we begin here

The next key question we must ask is, What kind of judges should we have? Today's federal judges have taken their belief in an evolving Constitution as license to act in ways not befitting the judicial branch. Simply put, modern judges legislate from the bench and impose their will on Congress, the president, and the American people in ways never intended by our Constitution. This concept of judicial supremacy has given judges the final say in the meaning of every societal question through their interpretation of an evolving Constitution. In essence, the courts are remaking society in their image. A judicial conservative as expressed in the Scalia model has a more humble and constitutional view of the role of judges, which we explore in these pages.

The subsequent chapters each identify one issue area impacted by the Court. For each topic area, I have provided a brief overview to help place the item for discussion in some context. Then, the Scalia model is presented in Scalia's words – opinions offered while on the Supreme Court, as well as writings, speeches, and other published reports. Our task has been to compile the information and present it in a useable and understandable format. We have included a source reference for each quote, while our rule has been to omit internal references for ease of reading. Of course, these references are available simply by accessing the original sources. I have also included a related quote from the writings and statements of Samuel Alito for each of the 21 issues to offer perspective on Alito's judicial philosophy.

The first four topics cover the foundation stones of the judicial conservative philosophy: the view of the Constitution, the role the courts, separation of powers, and states' rights. Next, we tackle some core issues such as free exercise/establishment of religion, life/death and abortion, free speech, right to die, crime and punishment, and the death penalty. We then proceed to a discussion of welfare, affirmative action, and the color-blind society, as understood in the Scalia model.

From homosexuality to marriage to public decency, the courts have with increasing frequency weighed in on the core cultural issues facing our society. Therefore, we wanted to offer clarity on how a judicial conservative legal perspective addresses these issue. The reader may be surprised to discover that, in our opinion and following the Scalia model, judicial conservative judges and justices should extract themselves from these cultural debates. In *Lawrence v. Texas*, Scalia lamented, "It is clear from this [ruling] that the Court has taken sides in the culture war, departing from its role of assuring, as a neutral observer, that the democratic rules of engagement are observed."

Scalia is quite consistent in this position. For example, regarding abortion, Scalia has said, "I will strike down *Roe v. Wade*, but I will also strike down a law that is the opposite of *Roe v. Wade*. ... One [side] wants no state to be able to prohibit abortion and the other [side] wants every state to have to prohibit abortion, and they're both wrong, not because of my religious views but because that's how I read the Constitution." Although Grassfire.org is a conservative organization, we agree with Scalia's contention that the Court needs to extract itself from the culture war. Let the public debate begin again without the ominous overtone of a judiciary that seeks to impose its view of morality on society.

The next collection of subjects details judicial conservative thought as applied to issues impacting terrorism, war, and our nation's legal sovereignty. The judicial activism of late not only brings into question whether America will have the legal authority to conduct a successful war on terror, but whether U.S. law or the laws of other nations will ultimately rule us. These are additional reasons why the composition of the Supreme Court impacts the everyday lives of Americans more today than perhaps at any time in history.

The final subject matter discussed involves recent comments by Scalia regarding the politicization of the judicial confirmation process. In 1986, Antonin Scalia was confirmed by a vote of 98-0. Two senators were not present, so in effect he was confirmed 100-0. Less than two decades later, despite the fact that Scalia is regarded as one of the intellectual giants in American jurisprudence, most pundits said he would have faced a difficult confirmation battle if President Bush had selected him as chief justice.

The situation is the same for Samuel Alito, who was confirmed unanimously by the Senate to serve as a Circuit Court judge yet is facing mounting opposition. Alito has distinguished himself in his service to our country in the judiciary. He has honestly and forthrightly expressed his judicial philosophy in his writings and opinions, as demonstrated in this book. He should be confirmed.

I am grateful to Sean Rushton and the Committee For Justice (committeeforjustice.org) for honoring my request to include CFJ's assessment of Samuel Alito's legal positions as an Appendix to this document. Sean and CFJ have done a marvelous job in outlining Alito's philosophy and answering the Left's challenges. I encourage you to read this document and also to visit CFJ for more information on the judicial nomination process.

In closing, let me offer a personal anecdote as to why you are holding this unique book in your hands. On the eve of Election Day 2004, a friend of mine tried to offer some perspective on the uncertain presidential race. As a conservative, I was pulling strong and hard for George W. Bush to be re-elected to a second term. Just a few hours before Americans would begin casting their ballots, I emphasized to my friend, as I had done hundreds of times over the preceding weeks, just how important this election was. My friend tried to bring perspective: "We'll survive a Kerry presidency," he said. Of course, he was right. That's the wonder and majesty of the American experiment. America survives and even thrives whether your guy is in the White House or not.

But then my thoughts jumped quickly to the real issue at stake – the future of the federal courts in general and, more specifically, the Supreme Court. A Kerry presidency would have extended the reign of the imperial court by decades – perhaps into my own retirement. A Bush presidency would at least create an opportunity to see order restored to the courts and the great cultural questions of our day returned to the people.

That is my heart's desire. Two decades ago, President Ronald Reagan heralded "a time of renewal in the great constitutional system that our forefathers gave us." I believe what President Reagan saw then now has an opportunity to come to full blossom. And so we offer the *21 Supreme Court Issues Facing America* — our 21 reasons why every American should be deeply concerned about the Supreme Court. I hope this book will equip grassroots citizens to stand against tide of judicial activism with the confidence that we are standing with the stronger tide of history.

CHAPTER 1

Restoring the Constitution

A judicial conservative contends for the original meaning of the Constitution as the only secure foundation of a free society.

[T]he Constitution that I interpret and apply is not living, but dead; or as I prefer to call it, enduring. It means today not what current society, much less the Court, thinks it ought to mean, but what it meant when it was adopted.

Justice Antonin Scalia, January 25, 2002

Now if that's the kind of judge I was, I would certainly think that my ethical and moral and religious views would have a lot to do with my decisions. But I am not that kind of a judge. I look at text. I take my best shot at getting the fairest meaning of that text, and where it is a constitutional text, understanding what it meant at the time it was adopted.

Justice Antonin Scalia, January 25, 2002

Federal judges have the duty to interpret the Constitution and the laws faithfully and fairly, to protect the constitutional rights of all Americans, and to do these things with care and with restraint, always keeping in mind the limited role that the courts play in our constitutional system.

Judge Samuel Alito, October 31, 2005

L ex Rex. The Law is King. It's the fundamental legal principle of Western civilization and of the American experiment. The sources of our liberties can be traced back hundreds of years before our Constitution to this tantamount struggle between Rex and Lex, between what man would impose and what a written document would secure. British subjects and later American colonists would time and time again point to written documents to hold the power of the king in check and to secure their rights. Upon this foundation, the first generation of American citizens set out to establish Lex Rex through the development of a written Constitution, confirmed by the representatives of the states and binding on all. This legal document had a specific, permanent meaning, evidenced by the fact that an amendment process was established whereby the people could alter the meaning of the document. In America, Lex Rex, the Law is King, and the final law is our written Constitution.

Since about 1950, American jurisprudence has taken a frightening turn. The Constitution has become a living document whose meaning depends on the so-called "evolving standards" of society, not what the words actually state. This is the consensus view of not only our courts but academia, the mainstream media, and millions of Americans. Of these "21 Issues," none is more paramount than the fundamental view of the Constitution a judge or justice brings to the debate. A judicial conservative begins here – with a high viewå of the Constitution and a desire to uphold its original meaning as the only secure foundation for a free society. Justice Antonin Scalia's body of work clearly establishes an originalist model for conservative judges and justices, including Samuel Alito. Since every other issue we will discuss flows out of this first question—what does the Constitution mean?—let's explore the originalist view as presented in the Scalia model as a benchmark for understanding Judge Alito. —S.E.

The Scalia Model on Restoring the Constitution

Scalia is a textualist, originalist

I belong to a school, a small but hardy school, called "textualists" or "originalists." That used to be "constitutional orthodoxy" in the United States. The theory of originalism treats a constitution like a statute and gives it the meaning that its words were understood to bear at the time they were promulgated. ... You will never hear me refer to original intent, because as I say I am first of all a textualist, and secondly an originalist. If you are a textualist, you don't care about the intent.... I take the words as they were promulgated to the people of the United States, and what is the fairly understood meaning of those words....
(Remarks at the Catholic University of America, Washington, DC, 10/18/96)

Bear in mind that I don't make up new constitutional rules. [For example] I don't sit back and say should there be a right to die. You know, it's not really there in the Constitution, but you know, we have an evolving Constitution and maybe it ought to be there. Now, if that's the kind of judge I was, I would certainly think that my ethical and moral and religious views would have a lot to do with my decisions. But I am not that kind of a judge. I look at a text. I take my best shot at getting the fairest meaning of that text, and where it is a constitutional text, understanding what it meant at the time it was adopted. (Remarks at Pew Forum Conference, Chicago, IL, 1/25/02)

Scalia gives history of "originalism"

I am one of a small number of judges, small number of anybody — judges, professors, lawyers — who are known as originalists. Our manner of interpreting the Constitution is to begin with the text, and to give that text the meaning that it bore when it was adopted by the people. I'm not a "strict constructionist," despite the introduction. I don't like the term "strict construction." I do not think the Constitution, or any text, should be interpreted either strictly or sloppily; it should be interpreted reasonably. Many of my interpretations do not deserve the description "strict." I do believe, however, that you give the text the meaning it had when it was adopted.

This is such a minority position in modern academia and in modern legal circles that on occasion I'm asked when I've given a talk like this a question from the back of the room — "Justice Scalia, when did you first become an originalist?" — as though it is some kind of weird affliction that seizes some people — "When did you first start eating human flesh?"

Although it is a minority view now, the reality is that, not very long ago, originalism was orthodoxy. Everybody at least purported to be an originalist. If you go back and read the commentaries on the Constitution by Joseph Story, he didn't think the Constitution evolved or changed. He said it means and will always mean what it meant when it was adopted.

Or consider the opinions of John Marshall in the Federal Bank case, where he says, we must not, we must always remember it is a constitution we are expounding. And since it's a constitution, he says, you have to give its provisions expansive meaning so that they will accommodate events that you do not know of which will happen in the future.

Well, if it is a constitution that changes, you wouldn't have to give it an expansive meaning. You can give it whatever meaning you want and, when future necessity arises, you simply change the meaning. But anyway, that is no longer the orthodoxy.

Oh, one other example about how not just the judges and scholars believed in originalism, but even the American people. Consider the 19th Amendment, which is the amendment that gave women the vote. It was adopted by the American people in 1920. Why did we adopt a constitutional amendment for that purpose? The Equal Protection Clause existed in 1920; it was adopted right after the Civil War. And you know that if the issue of the franchise for women came up today, we would not have to have a constitutional amendment. Someone would come to the Supreme Court and say, "Your Honors, in a democracy, what could be a greater denial of equal protection than denial of the franchise?" And the Court would say, "Yes! Even though it never meant it before, the Equal Protection Clause means that women have to have the vote." But that's not how the American people thought in 1920. In 1920, they looked at the Equal Protection Clause and said, "What does it mean?" Well, it clearly doesn't mean that you can't discriminate in the franchise — not only on the basis of sex, but on the basis of property ownership, on the basis of literacy. None of that is unconstitutional. And therefore, since it wasn't unconstitutional, and we wanted it to be, we did things the good old-fashioned way and adopted an amendment.

Now, in asserting that originalism used to be orthodoxy, I do not mean to imply that judges did not distort the Constitution now and then, of course they did. We had willful judges then, and we will have willful judges until the end of time. But the difference is that prior to the last 50 years or so, prior to the advent of the "living Constitution," judges did their distortions the good old-fashioned way, the honest way — they lied about it. They said the Constitution means such and such, when it never meant such and such. (Remarks at the Woodrow Wilson Center, Washington, DC, 3/14/05)

Scalia "handcuffed" by originalism

I have my rules that confine me. I know what I'm looking for. When I find it — the original meaning of the Constitution — I am handcuffed. If I believe that the First Amendment meant when it was adopted that you are entitled to burn the American flag, I have to come out that way even though I don't like to come out that way. When I find that the original meaning of the jury trial guarantee is that any additional time you spend in prison which depends upon a fact must depend upon a fact found by a jury — once I find that's what the jury trial guarantee means, I am handcuffed. Though I'm a law-and-order type, I cannot do all the mean conservative things I would like to do to this society. You got me. (Remarks at the Woodrow Wilson Center, Washington, DC, 3/14/05)

Constitution is "not living," "anchor...rock"

[T]he Constitution that I interpret and apply is not living, but dead; or as I prefer to call it, enduring. It means today not what current society, much less the Court, thinks it ought to mean, but what it meant when it was adopted. (Remarks at Pew Forum Conference, Chicago, IL, 1/25/02)

The words are the law. ... We are bound not by the intent of our legislators, but by the laws which they enacted, which are set forth in words, of course. ... [T]he Constitution was that anchor, that rock, that unchanging institution that forms the American polity. ... What it meant when it was adopted it means today, and its meaning doesn't change just because we think that meaning is no longer adequate to our times. If it's inadequate, we can amend it.... (Remarks at the Catholic University of America, Washington, DC, 10/18/96)

In a system based upon constitutional and statutory text democratically adopted, the concept of 'law' ordinarily signifies that particular words have a fixed meaning. Such law does not change, and this Court's pronouncement of it therefore remains authoritative until (confessing our prior error) we overrule. (*Roper v. Simmons*, 112 S. W. 3d 397, affirmed, [2005])

Countering the "evolving standards" argument

[A]ll this development, away from originalism, has occurred within the past 40 years. Today, we say in our opinions, We believe, the Court believes, and worst of all the American people believe that not only the Eighth Amendment but the whole Bill of Rights, the whole Constitution, "reflects the evolving standards of decency of a maturing society." Or, to put it more simply, the Constitution means what it ought to mean. Not what it did mean, but what it ought to mean. And so, all sorts of rights that clearly did not exist at the time of the Constitution today. (Remarks at the Catholic University of America, Washington, DC, 10/18/96)

It should not be thought, although it is often argued, that this new way of looking at the Constitution is desirable because it promotes needed flexibility. ... The argument is 'The Constitution is meant for a living society. If it could not grow and evolve with the society, it would become brittle and snap. You have to provide the flexibility.' ... [But w]hat was the situation before *Roe v. Wade*? If you wanted a right to an abortion, create that right the way a democratic society creates most rights. Pass a law. If you don't want it, pass a law against it. ... That's flexibility. (Remarks at the Catholic University of America, Washington, DC, 10/18/96)

If the Eighth Amendment set forth an ordinary rule of law, it would indeed be the role of this Court to say what the law is. But the Court having pronounced that the Eighth Amendment is an ever-changing reflection of "the evolving standards of decency" of our society, it makes no sense for the Justices then to prescribe those standards rather than discern them from the practices of our people. On the evolving-standards hypothesis, the only legitimate function of this Court is to identify a moral consensus of the American people. By what conceivable warrant can nine lawyers presume to be the authoritative conscience of the Nation? (*Roper v. Simmons*, 112 S. W. 3d 397, affirmed, [2005])

Well, you know maybe 60 years or so ago we adopted, first in the Eighth Amendment area, cruel and unusual punishment the notion that the Constitution is not static. It doesn't mean what the people voted for when it was ratified. It doesn't mean that. Rather, it changes from era to era to comport with — and this is a quote from our cases, "the evolving standards of decency that mark the progress of a maturing society." I detest that phrase ... because I'm afraid that societies don't always mature. Sometimes they rot. What makes you think that, you know, human progress is one upwardly inclined plane, every day and every way we get better and better? It seems to me that the purpose of the Bill of Rights was to prevent change, not to encourage it and have it written into a Constitution. (Remarks at U.S. Association of Constitutional Law Discussion, Washington, DC, 1/13/05)

Constitution changed through amendments

[The proper way of thinking] is demonstrated by the 19th Amendment, adopted in 1920. That is the amendment which guaranteed women the right to vote. As you know, there was a national campaign of "suffragettes" to get this constitutional amendment adopted.... Why did they go through all that trouble? If people then thought the way people think now, there would have been no need. There was an Equal Protection Clause, right there in the Constitution in 1920. ... And so why didn't these people just come to the Court and say, "This is a denial of equal protection"? Because they didn't think that way. Equal protection could mean that everybody has to have the vote. ... It could mean a lot of things in the abstract. It could meant that women must be sent into combat, for example. It could meant that have to have unisex toilets in public buildings. But does it mean those things? ... That was not its understood meaning. And since that was not its meaning in 1871, it's not its meaning today.... (Remarks at the Catholic University of America, Washington, DC, 10/18/96)

Describing the current "living Constitution" view

It's a big difference that you now no longer have to lie about [what the Constitution means], because we are in the era of the evolving Constitution. And the judge can simply say, "Oh yes, the Constitution didn't used to mean that, but it does now." We are in the age in which not only judges, not only lawyers, but even schoolchildren have come to learn the Constitution changes. I have grammar school students come into the Court now and then, and they recite very proudly what they have been taught: "The Constitution is a living document." You know, it morphs. (Remarks at the Woodrow Wilson Center, Washington, DC, 3/14/05)

What are the arguments usually made in favor of the Living Constitution? As the name of it suggests, it is a very attractive philosophy, and it's hard to talk people out of it — the notion that the Constitution grows. The major argument is the Constitution is a living organism, it has to grow with the society that it governs or it will become brittle and snap. This is the equivalent of, an anthropomorphism equivalent to what you hear from your stockbroker, when he tells you that the stock market is resting for an assault on the 11,000 level. The stock market panting at some base camp. The stock market is not a mountain climber and the Constitution is not a living organism for Pete's sake; it's a legal document, and like all legal documents, it says some things, and it doesn't say other things. And if you think that the aficionados of the Living Constitution want to bring you flexibility, think again. (Remarks at the Woodrow Wilson Center, Washington, DC, 3/14/05)

Living Constitution does not promote more freedoms

Some people are in favor of the Living Constitution because they think it always leads to greater freedom — there's just nothing to lose, the evolving Constitution will always provide greater and greater freedom, more and more rights. Why would you think that? It's a two-way street. And indeed, under the aegis of the Living Constitution, some freedoms have been taken away. (Remarks at the Woodrow Wilson Center, Washington, DC, 3/14/05)

Not a liberal/conservative debate

That's not the name of the game. Some people also seem to like it because they think it's a good liberal thing — that somehow this is a conservative/liberal battle, and conservatives like the old-fashioned originalist Constitution and liberals ought to like the Living Constitution. That's not true either. The dividing line between those who believe in the Living Constitution and those who don't is not the dividing line between conservatives and liberals.

Conservatives are willing to grow the Constitution to cover their favorite causes just as liberals are, and the best example of that is two cases we announced some years ago on the same day, the same morning. One case was *Romer v. Evans*, in which the people of Colorado had enacted an amendment to the state constitution by plebiscite, which said that neither the state nor any subdivision of the state would add to the protected statuses against which private individuals cannot discriminate. The usual ones are race, religion, age, sex, disability, and so forth. Would not add sexual preference — somebody thought that was a terrible idea, and, since it was a terrible idea, it must be unconstitutional. Brought a lawsuit, it came to the

Supreme Court. And the Supreme Court said, "Yes, it is unconstitutional." On the basis of — I don't know. The Sexual Preference Clause of the Bill of Rights, presumably. And the liberals loved it, and the conservatives gnashed their teeth.

The very next case we announce is a case called *BMW v. [Gore]*. Not the [Gore] you think; this is another [Gore]. Mr. [Gore] had bought a BMW, which is a car supposedly advertised at least as having a superb finish, baked seven times in ovens deep in the Alps, by dwarfs. And his BMW apparently had gotten scratched on the way over. They did not send it back to the Alps, they took a can of spray-paint and fixed it. And he found out about this and was furious, and he brought a lawsuit. He got his compensatory damages, a couple of hundred dollars — the difference between a car with a better paint job and a worse paint job — plus $2 million against BMW for punitive damages for being a bad actor, which is absurd of course, so it must be unconstitutional. BMW appealed to my Court, and my Court said, "Yes, it's unconstitutional." In violation of, I assume, the Excessive Damages Clause of the Bill of Rights. And if excessive punitive damages are unconstitutional, why aren't excessive compensatory damages unconstitutional? So you have a federal question whenever you get a judgment in a civil case. Well, that one the conservatives liked, because conservatives don't like punitive damages, and the liberals gnashed their teeth.

I dissented in both cases because I say, "A pox on both their houses." It has nothing to do with what your policy preferences are; it has to do with what you think the Constitution is. (Remarks at the Woodrow Wilson Center, Washington, DC, 3/14/05)

The "death knell" of the Constitution

[N]on-originalism ... is the death knell of the Constitution. ... [T]he whole purpose of the Constitution is to prevent a future society from doing what it wants to do. ... To change, to evolve, you don't need a Constitution, all you need is a legislature and a ballot box. ... The only reason you need a Constitution is because some things you don't want the majority to be able to change. That's my most important function as a judge in this system. I have to tell the majority to take a hike. I tell them, "I don't care what you want, but the Bill of Rights says you cannot do it." Now if there is no fixed absolute ... a majority of the people will look for judges who agree with them as to what the Constitution means. ... We are conducting a mini-plebiscite on the meaning of the Constitution every time we select a new person for the Supreme Court. Isn't that what's happening? Does it make any sense? But I suggest that is the inevitable result if you abandon originalism and move to a constitution that means what it ought to mean. ...

What did its words mean when they were adopted? I think we depart from the traditional view of the Constitution at our own risk. ... We've only been doing it for 40 years. We haven't lasted for 200 years doing it. And we haven't gone far down the road. I think at the end of it, at the end of the road, there is really a serious weakening of constitutional democracy. (Remarks at the Catholic University of America, Washington, DC, 10/18/96)

CHAPTER 2

Ending Judicial Supremacy

A judicial conservative contends to restore the constitutional role of the courts and end the doctrine of judicial supremacy.

What these people want is to impose a view of things on the whole society from coast to coast, and it is most quickly and most effectively done through the Constitution. … The Constitution nowhere says that the Supreme Court shall be the last word on what the Constitution means.

Justice Antonin Scalia, January 25, 2002

"Most of the labels people use to talk about judges, and the way judges decide (cases) aren't too descriptive. … Judges should be judges. They shouldn't be legislators, they shouldn't be administrators."

Samuel Alito, 2005

A rmed with an "evolving" or "living" Constitution, liberal activists have sought to re-make society in their own image. They have had some success using the executive and legislative branches but have faced the constraint of elections and public accountability. The courts – the branch which historically has been least threatening to the rights of the people – became the perfect avenue for change because federal judges never face election. Since the middle of the 20th century, a doctrine of judicial supremacy has been promoted in which judges have the final say in the meaning of every societal question through their interpretation of an evolving Constitution. Judges have taken this license to, through their opinions, in essence write the equivalent of legislation and demand enforcement of their pronouncements. Thus, the courts now have final judicial, legislative, and executive power – the courts have become king.

As noted, a judicial conservative has a different perpsective of the Constitution, viewing it as a fixed document with a fixed meaning. Likewise, a judicial conservative draws from that document a fixed and limited view of the role of the courts. As we see in the Scalia model, such a judge opposes an imperial court and the doctrine of judicial supremacy on all societal matters. The challenge facing nominees such as Samuel Alito is to restore the proper constitutional role of the courts and end judicial supremacy in America. How does Alito measure up to the Scalia model of the court's role in our society? First, let's explore the Scalia model. —S.E.

The Scalia Model on Ending Judicial Supremacy

Understanding of Judicial Review

The only reason federal courts sit in judgment of the constitutionality of federal legislation is not because they are explicitly authorized to do so in the Constitution. Some modern constitutions give the constitutional court explicit authority to review German legislation or French legislation for its constitutionality, [but] our Constitution doesn't say anything like that. But John Marshall says in *Marbury v. Madison*: Look, this is lawyers' work. What you have here is an apparent conflict between the Constitution and the statute. And, all the time, lawyers and judges have to reconcile these conflicts — they try to read the two to comport with each other. If they can't, it's judges' work to decide which ones prevail. When there are two statutes, the more recent one prevails. It implicitly repeals the older one. But when the Constitution is at issue, the Constitution prevails because it is a "superstatute." I mean, that's what Marshall says: It's judges' work. (Remarks at the Woodrow Wilson Center, Washington, DC, 3/14/05)

So these people who go around talking about the need for growing and bending — that's nonsense. What these people want is to impose a view of things on the whole society from coast to coast, and it is most quickly and most effectively done through the Constitution. ... The Constitution of the United States nowhere says that the Supreme Court shall be the last word on what the Constitution means. Or that the Supreme Court shall have the authority to disregard statutes enacted by the Congress of the United States on the ground that in its view they do not comport with the Constitution." (Remarks at Pew Forum Conference, Chicago, IL, 1/25/02)

Scalia recently described in three steps the process of judicial supremacy, or the judicial usurpation of the Constitution through the application of a so-called "living Constitution."

Step One: Give terms in the Constitution a new meaning

Initially, the Court began giving terms in the text of the Constitution a meaning they didn't have when they were adopted. For example, the First Amendment, which forbids Congress to abridge the freedom of speech. What does the freedom of speech mean? Well, it clearly did not mean that Congress or government could not impose any restrictions upon speech. Libel laws, for example, were clearly constitutional. Nobody thought the First Amendment was *carte blanche* to libel someone. But in the famous case of *New York Times v. Sullivan* , the Supreme Court said, "But the First Amendment does prevent you from suing for libel if you are a public figure and if the libel was not malicious" — that is, the person, a member of the press or otherwise, thought that what the person said was true. Well, that had never been the law. I mean, it might be a good law. And some states could amend their libel law....It's one thing for a state to amend its libel law and say, "We think that public figures shouldn't be able to sue." That's fine. But the courts have said that the First Amendment, which never meant this before, now means that if you are a public figure, that you can't sue for libel unless it's intentional, malicious. So that's one way to do it.

Another example is the Constitution guarantees the right to be represented by counsel. That never meant the state had to pay for your counsel. But you can reinterpret it to mean that. (Remarks at the Woodrow Wilson Center, Washington, DC, 3/14/05)

Step Two: Substantive due process with limitations

[Step One] will only get you so far. There is no text in the Constitution that you could reinterpret to create a right to abortion, for example. So you need something else. The something else is called the doctrine of "Substantive Due Process." Only lawyers can walk around talking about substantive process, inasmuch as it's a contradiction in terms. If you referred to substantive process or procedural substance at a cocktail party, people would look at you funny. But lawyers talk this way all the time.

What substantive due process is is quite simple — the Constitution has a Due Process Clause, which says that no person shall be deprived of life, liberty or property without due process of law. Now, what does this guarantee? Does it guarantee life, liberty or property? No, indeed! All three can be taken away. You can be fined, you can be incarcerated, you can even be executed, but not without due process of law. It's a procedural guarantee. But the Court said, and this goes way back, in the 1920s at least, in fact the first case to do it was Dred Scott. But it became more popular in the 1920s. The Court said there are some liberties that are so important, that no process will suffice to take them away. Hence, substantive due process.

Now, what liberties are they? The Court will tell you. Be patient. When the doctrine of substantive due process was initially announced, it was limited in this way: The Court said it embraces only those liberties that are fundamental to a democratic society and rooted in the traditions of the American people. (Remarks at the Woodrow Wilson Center, Washington, DC, 3/14/05)

Step Three: Liberation from the Constitution

Then we come to step three… that limitation is eliminated. Within the last 20 years, we have found to be covered by due process the right to abortion, which was so little rooted in the traditions of the American people that it was criminal for 200 years; the right to homosexual sodomy, which was so little rooted in the traditions of the American people that it was criminal for 200 years. So it is literally true, and I don't think this is an exaggeration, that the Court has essentially liberated itself from the text of the Constitution, from the text and even from the traditions of the American people. It is up to the Court to say what is covered by substantive due process. (Remarks at the Woodrow Wilson Center, Washington, DC, 3/14/05)

Judges should not rewrite the laws; people should

[A judge has] taken an oath to apply those laws and has been given no power to supplant them with rules of his own. Of course, if he feels strongly enough, he can go beyond mere resignation and lead a political campaign to abolish the death penalty, and if that fails, lead a revolution. But rewrite the laws he cannot do. This dilemma, of course, need not be faced by proponents of the living Constitution who believe that it means what it ought to mean…You can see why the living Constitution has such attraction for us judges. (Remarks at Pew Forum Conference, Chicago, IL, 1/25/02)

What binds the biases of a judge? Prevents him from simply implementing his own prejudices? What is the standard? …The answer is, there isn't any. …

It is indeed true that "later generations can see that laws once thought necessary and proper in fact serve only to oppress," and when that happens, later generations can repeal those laws. But it is the premise of our system that those judgments are to be made by the people, and not imposed by a governing caste that knows best. (*Lawrence v. Texas*, 41 S. W. 3d 349, reversed and remanded [2003])

Judges unfit to determine "evolving standards"

If you believe… that the Constitution is not a legal text, like the texts involved when judges reconcile or decide which of two statutes prevail; if you think the Constitution is some exhortation to give effect to the most fundamental values of the society as those values change from year to year; if you think that it is meant to reflect, as some of the Supreme Court cases say, particularly those involving the Eighth Amendment, if you think it is simply meant to reflect the evolving standards of decency that mark the progress of a maturing society — if that is what you think it is, then why in the world would you have it interpreted by nine lawyers? What do I know about the evolving standards of decency of American society? I'm afraid to ask.

If that is what you think the Constitution is, then *Marbury v. Madison* is wrong. It shouldn't be up to the judges, it should be up to the legislature. We should have a system like the English — whatever the legislature thinks is constitutional is constitutional. They know the evolving standards of American society, I don't. So in principle, it's incompatible with the legal regime that America has established. (Remarks at the Woodrow Wilson Center, Washington, DC, 3/14/05)

Living Constitution judges "make these decisions for us"

Now, if you're not going to control your judges that way, what other criterion are you going to place before them? What is the criterion that governs the Living Constitutional judge? What can you possibly use, besides original meaning? Think about that. Natural law? We all agree on that, don't we? The philosophy of John Rawls? That's easy. There really is nothing else. You either tell your judges, "Look, this is a law, like all laws. Give it the meaning it had when it was adopted." Or, you tell your judges, "Govern us. You tell us whether people under 18, who committed their crimes when they were under 18, should be executed. You tell us whether there ought to be an unlimited right to abortion or a partial right to abortion. You make these decisions for us." I have put this question — you know I speak at law schools with some frequency just to make trouble — and I put this question to the faculty all the time, or incite the students to ask their Living Constitutional professors: "Okay, professor, you are not an originalist. What is your criterion?" There is none other. (Remarks at the Woodrow Wilson Center, Washington, DC, 3/14/05)

Today's opinion shows more forcefully than volumes of argumentation why our Nation's protection, that fortress which is our Constitution, cannot possibly rest upon the changeable philosophical predilections of the Justices of this Court, but must have deep foundations in the historic practices of our people. (*Lee v. Weisman*, 505 U.S. 577 [1992])

Protecting against majoritarian rule

My most important function on the Supreme Court is to tell the majority to take a walk. And the notion that the justices ought to be selected because of the positions that they will take, that are favored by the majority, is a recipe for destruction of what we have had for 200 years…. This is new — 50 years old or so — the Living Constitution stuff. We have not yet seen what the end of the road is. I think we are beginning to see. And what it is should really be troublesome to Americans who care about a Constitution that can provide protections against majoritarian rule. (Remarks at the Woodrow Wilson Center, Washington, DC, 3/14/05)

CHAPTER 3

Upholding Separation of Powers

A judicial conservative works to re-establish the separation of powers principle in our Constitution.

This statute...does substantially affect the balance of powers. That the Court could possibly conclude otherwise demonstrates both the wisdom of our former constitutional system and the folly of the new system of standardless judicial allocation of powers we adopt today.
Justice Antonin Scalia, *Morrison v. Olson*, 1988

"In the field of law, I disagree strenuously with the usurpation by the judiciary of decisionmaking authority that should be exercised by the branches of government responsible to the electorate."
Samuel Alito, 1985

*T*he U.S. Constitution, by its very structure, establishes at its outset the vital principle of separation of powers. The first three Articles clearly lay out the legislative, executive, and judicial powers. This principle of separation of powers is a central feature of the republican form of government in the United States and is designed to both protect and keep in check each of the three branches of government.

Today, led by the courts, the lines of power have been blurred. Instead of following the Constitution's model of separation of powers, we now have, as Antonin Scalia has noted, "judicial allocation of powers." This is not the Scalia model for a conservative jurist. Instead, a judicial conservative must be a strong proponent of separation of powers who will uphold the proper, constitutionally allocated power of the legislative, executive, and judicial branches. Antonin Scalia stated his view on this topic most clearly in Morrison v. Olson, *which involved a congressional investigation of the executive branch by an independent counsel. The independent counsel was given full force of prosecutorial powers, and Scalia argued this was a usurpation of executive powers by the Congress. Let us explore the Scalia model of separation of powers and then consider Alito's views on the subject.* —S.E.

The Scalia Model on Upholding Separation of Powers

Preserving the equilibrium

That is what this suit is about. Power. The allocation of power among Congress, the President, and the courts in such fashion as to preserve the equilibrium the Constitution sought to establish — so that "a gradual concentration of the several powers in the same department" can effectively be resisted.…

The present case began when the Legislative and Executive Branches became "embroiled in a dispute concerning the scope of the congressional investigatory power," which — as is often the case with such interbranch conflicts — became quite acrimonious. In the course of oversight hearings into the administration of the Superfund by the Environmental Protection Agency (EPA), two Subcommittees of the House of Representatives requested and then subpoenaed numerous internal EPA documents. The President responded by personally directing the EPA Administrator not to turn over certain of the documents, and by having the Attorney General notify the congressional Subcommittees of this assertion of executive privilege. (*Morrison v. Olson*, 487 U.S. 654 [1988])

Congress and the executive branch came to a compromise agreement; subcommittees were granted limited access to a small number of documents. However, the House Judiciary Committee investigated the controversy, and instructed the Attorney General to appoint an independent counsel to investigate the matter. According to the law under review, the Attorney General is compelled to appoint an independent counsel to investigate a member of the executive branch.

Thus, by the application of this statute in the present case, Congress has effectively compelled a criminal investigation of a high-level appointee of the President in connection with his actions arising out of a bitter power dispute between the President and the Legislative Branch. (*Morrison v. Olson*, 487 U.S. 654 [1988])

Opposing "standardless judicial allocation of powers"

To repeat, Article II, 1, cl. 1, of the Constitution provides: "The executive Power shall be vested in a President of the United States." As I described at the outset of this opinion, this does not mean some of the executive power, but all of the executive power. It seems to me, therefore, that the decision of the Court of Appeals invalidating the present statute must be upheld on fundamental separation-of-powers principles if the following two questions are answered affirmatively: (1) Is the conduct of a criminal prosecution (and of an investigation to decide whether to prosecute) the exercise of purely executive power? (2) Does the statute deprive the President of the United States of exclusive control over the exercise of that power? Surprising to say, the Court appears to concede an affirmative answer to both questions, but seeks to avoid the inevitable conclusion that since the statute vests some purely executive power in a person who is not the President of the United States it is void. ... In sum, this statute does deprive the President of substantial control over the prosecutory functions performed by the independent counsel, and it does substantially affect the balance of powers. That the Court could possibly conclude otherwise demonstrates both the wisdom of our former constitutional system, in which the degree of reduced control and political impairment were irrelevant, since all purely executive power had to be in the President; and the folly of the new system of standardless judicial allocation of powers we adopt today. (*Morrison v. Olson*, 487 U.S. 654 [1988])

CHAPTER 4

Affirming Dual Sovereignty and States' Rights

A judicial conservative works to restore the proper balance between federal and state authority.

*The Federal Government may neither issue directives requiring the States to
address particular problems, nor command the States' officers, or those of their
political subdivisions, to administer or enforce a federal regulatory
program...Such commands are fundamentally incompatible
with our constitutional system of dual sovereignty.*
Justice Antonin Scalia, *Printz v. United States,* 1997

*"The law of evidence recognizes many sensitive and important
nonconstitutional privileges.... Federal and state lawmakers have not
generally evinced hostility toward these other nonconstitutional privileges
but in fact in recent years have recognized a host of new privileges."*
Samuel Alito, 1988

---

*A*s clearly established by the 10th Amendment, the Founding Fathers
intended for the federal government to have strictly defined powers,
*leaving most questions of law and policy to the states. Some sixty years after
the ratification of the 14th Amendment, the Supreme Court began to use the
due process clause of that amendment (called "substantive due process") to
establish the "incorporation" principle to apply the Bill of Rights to the states.
Over time, the Court has used incorporation to create an impenetrable right
to "liberty" that it has used, at its discretion, to limit the rights of the states.*

*As a result, the Supreme Court has again and again struck down state
laws, disrupting the balance of power between the federal government and
the states so clearly established by the 10th Amendment – what Antonin
Scalia calls "dual sovereignty." Scalia has consistently argued against this
unaccountable extension of federal power at the whim of the courts and at
the expense of the states. This is the Scalia model that should guide judicial conservatives in our courts. Judicial nominees like Samuel Alito
should uphold the constitutional rights of the states within the principle of
dual sovereignty and oppose unlimited incorporation under the guise of an
unlimited right to liberty. —S.E.*

The Scalia Model on Affirming Dual Sovereignty and States' Rights

Dual (federal/state) sovereignty explained

It is incontestible that the Constitution established a system of "dual sovereignty." Although the States surrendered many of their powers to the new Federal Government, they retained "a residuary and inviolable sovereignty." This is reflected throughout the Constitution's text, including (to mention only a few examples) the prohibition on any involuntary reduction or combination of a State's territory, Art. IV, §3; the Judicial Power Clause, Art. III, §2, and the Privileges and Immunities Clause, Art. IV, §2, which speak of the "Citizens" of the States; the amendment provision, Article V, which requires the votes of three fourths of the States to amend the Constitution; and the Guarantee Clause, Art. IV, §4, which "presupposes the continued existence of the states and . . . those means and instrumentalities which are the creation of their sovereign and reserved rights." Residual state sovereignty was also implicit, of course, in the Constitution's conferral upon Congress of not all governmental powers, but only discrete, enumerated ones, Art. I, §8, which implication was rendered express by the Tenth Amendment's assertion that "[t]he powers not delegated to the United States by the Constitution, nor prohibited by it to the States, are reserved to the States respectively, or to the people."

The Framers' experience under the Articles of Confederation had persuaded them that using the States as the instruments of federal governance was both ineffectual and provocative of federal state conflict. Preservation of the States as independent political entities being the price of union, and "[t]he practicality of making laws, with coercive sanctions, for the States as political bodies" having been, in Madison's words, "exploded on all hands," Records of the Federal Convention of 1787, the Framers rejected the concept of a central government that would act upon and through the States, and instead designed a system in which the state and federal governments would exercise concurrent authority over the people — who were, in Hamilton's words, "the only proper objects of government," ... The great innovation of this design was that our citizens would have two political capacities, one state and one federal, each protected from incursion by the other.... The Constitution thus contemplates that a State's government will represent and remain accountable to its own citizens. ... This separation of the two spheres is one of the Constitution's structural protections of liberty....

We have thus far discussed the effect that federal control of state officers would have upon the first element of the "double security" alluded to by Madison: the division of power between State and Federal Governments. It would also have an effect upon the second element: the separation and equilibration of powers between the three branches of the Federal Government itself. The Constitution does not leave to speculation who is to administer the laws enacted by Congress; the President, it says, "shall take Care that the Laws be faithfully executed," Art. II, §3, personally and through officers whom he appoints (save for such inferior officers as Congress may authorize to be appointed by the "Courts of Law" or by "the Heads of Departments" who are themselves presidential appointees), Art. II, §2. The Brady Act effectively transfers this responsibility to thousands of CLEOs in the 50 States, who are left to implement the program without meaningful Presidential control (if indeed meaningful Presidential control is possible without the power to appoint and remove). The insistence of the Framers upon unity in the Federal Executive — to insure both vigor and accountability — is well known. That unity would be shattered, and the power of the President would be subject to reduction, if Congress could act as effectively without the President as with him, by simply requiring state officers to execute its laws. (*Printz v. United States*, 521 U.S. 898 [1997])

Limits to federal control over states

The Federal Government may neither issue directives requiring the States to address particular problems, nor command the States' officers, or those of their political subdivisions, to administer or enforce a federal regulatory program. It matters not whether policy-making is involved, and no case by case weighing of the burdens or benefits is necessary; such commands are fundamentally incompatible with our constitutional system of dual sovereignty. (*Printz v. United States,* 521 U.S. 898 [1997])

No "right to liberty" but right to due process

Texas Penal Code undoubtedly imposes constraints on liberty. So do laws prohibiting prostitution, recreational use of heroin, and, for that matter, working more than 60 hours per week in a bakery. But there is no right to "liberty" under the Due Process Clause, though today's opinion repeatedly makes that claim. ("The liberty protected by the Constitution allows homosexual persons the right to make this choice"); … ("Their right to liberty under the Due Process Clause gives them the full right to engage in their conduct without intervention of the government"). The Fourteenth Amendment expressly allows States to deprive their citizens of "liberty," so long as "due process of law" is provided: "No state shall … deprive any person of life, liberty, or property, without due process of law." (*Lawrence v. Texas,* 41 S. W. 3d 349, reversed and remanded [2003])

Change being forced on states

The people may decide to change the one tradition, like the other, through democratic processes; but the assertion that either tradition has been unconstitutional through the centuries is not law, but politics-smuggled-into-law. … Today, however, change is forced upon Virginia, and reversion to single-sex education is prohibited nationwide, not by democratic processes but by order of this Court. Even while bemoaning the sorry, bygone days of "fixed notions" concerning women's education, the Court favors current notions so fixedly that it is willing to write them into the Constitution of the United States by application of custom-built "tests." This is not the interpretation of a Constitution, but the creation of one. (*U.S. v. Virginia*, 518 U.S. 515 [1996])

States should decide "where reasonable people disagree"

The permissibility of abortion, and the limitations upon it, are to be resolved like most important questions in our democracy: by citizens trying to persuade one another and then voting. As the Court acknowledges, "where reasonable people disagree, the government can adopt one position or the other." The Court is correct in adding the qualification that this "assumes a state of affairs in which the choice does not intrude upon a protected liberty," but the crucial part of that qualification is the penultimate word. A State's choice between two positions on which reasonable people can disagree is constitutional even when (as is often the case) it intrudes upon a "liberty" in the absolute sense. Laws against bigamy, for example — which entire societies of reasonable people disagree with — intrude upon men and women's liberty to marry and live with one another. But bigamy happens not to be a liberty specially "protected" by the Constitution. (*Planned Parenthood v. Casey*, 505 U.S. 833 [1992])

States can decide on sexual mores

The Court has mistaken a Kulturkampf [struggle for self-government] for a fit of spite. The constitutional amendment before us here is not the manifestation of a "bare ... desire to harm" homosexuals, but is rather a modest attempt by seemingly tolerant Coloradans to preserve traditional sexual mores against the efforts of a politically powerful minority to revise those mores through use of the laws. That objective, and the means chosen to achieve it, are not only unimpeachable under any constitutional doctrine hitherto pronounced (hence the opinion's heavy reliance upon principles of righteousness rather than judicial holdings); they have been specifically approved by the Congress of the United States and by this Court." (*Romer v. Evans*, 517 U.S. 620 [1996])

But there is a much closer analogy, one that involves precisely the effort by the majority of citizens to preserve its view of sexual morality statewide, against the efforts of a geographically concentrated and politically powerful minority to undermine it. The constitutions of the States of Arizona, Idaho, New Mexico, Oklahoma, and Utah to this day contain provisions stating that polygamy is "forever prohibited." Polygamists, and those who have a polygamous "orientation," have been "singled out" by these provisions for much more severe treatment than merely denial of favored status; and that treatment can only be changed by achieving amendment of the state constitutions. The Court's disposition today suggests that these provisions are unconstitutional, and that polygamy must be permitted in these States on a state-legislated, or perhaps even local-option, basis — unless, of course, polygamists for some reason have fewer constitutional rights than homosexuals. (*Romer v. Evans*, 517 U.S. 620 [1996])

Constitution, not personal views, must decide

As I made clear in my remarks, I will strike down *Roe v. Wade*, but I will also strike down a law that is the opposite of *Roe v. Wade*. You know, both sides in that debate want the Supreme Court to decide the matter for them. One wants no state to be able to prohibit abortion and the other one wants every state to have to prohibit abortion, and they're both wrong, not because of my religious views but because that's how I read the Constitution. It says nothing on the subject, whatever my religious views on the subject are, and I have religious views on the subject. But they have nothing whatever to do with my job. (Remarks at Pew Forum Conference, Chicago, IL, 1/25/02)

CHAPTER 5

Upholding Public Acknowledgment of God

Judges and justices should defend the people's right to honor our religious heritage and publicly acknowledge God.

The founding fathers never used the phrase "separation of church and state."
Justice Antonin Scalia, November 22, 2004

Applying these precedents, we see no endorsement [of religion] problem here. Child
Evangelism's flyers specifically disclaim any school sponsorship.."
Samuel Alito, majority opinion, *Child Evangelism Fellowship v. Stafford* (2004)

The Supreme Court's decisions regarding holiday displays have been marked by fine line-
drawing, and therefore it is not easy to determine whether particular displays satisfy the
Court's standards. …Reasonably viewed, none of these displays conveyed a message of
government endorsement of Christianity, Judaism, or of religion in general."
Samuel Alito, majority opinion, *ACLU v. Schundler,* 1999

"*C*ongress shall make no law respecting an establishment of religion or prohibiting the free exercise thereof." These first 16
words of our First Amendment have caused countless hours of debate and
volumes of court opinions. About a half century ago, the interpretation of
the meaning of these words began to change dramatically, beginning with
the insertion by Justice Black the words "separation of church and state"
(Everson v. Board of Education, 1947) – words not found in the
Constitution – into our jurisprudence. Today, the Court has imposed a
mandate of neutrality in its application of the Establishment clause under
the flawed and confusing "Lemon" test and the coercion test. The result has
been a growing hostility to religion in our courts and a mandate of a secular public culture.

Antonin Scalia strongly disagrees with the supposed mandate of government neutrality that creates what Richard John Neuhaus called a "naked
public square." He also opposes the Lemon test and argues that although the
Constitution prohibits the establishment of a state religion, it does not
mandate the destruction of our religious heritage. To the contrary: America
is a religious country, according to Scalia, and the First Amendment was

not intended to destroy the customs of American society. This is the Scalia model, only controversial in our current climate of religious hostility. Samuel Alito's track record indicates that he will uphold the right of the people to honor our nation's religious heritage as well as the acknowledgment of God by public officials and in public places. Let's look at the Scalia model and Alito's views. —S.E.

The Scalia Model on Upholding Public Acknowledgment of God

America "presupposes a supreme being"

It seems to me that the reaction of people of faith to this tendency of democracy to obscure the divine authority behind government should be not resignation to it but resolution to combat it as effectively as possible, and a principal way of combating it, in my view, is constant public reminder that — in the words of one of the Supreme Court's religion cases in the days when we understood the religion clauses better than I think we now do — "we are a religious people whose institutions presuppose a supreme being." We continue to do this, to make these public reminders in the United States in a number of ways: the annual Thanksgiving proclamation that has been issued ever since George Washington, for example; the ministers in the Congress and in the state legislative bodies; and for that matter, the opening of my court, "God save the United States and this Honorable Court." That is one way, by the way, in which we differ significantly from the thoroughly secularized European countries. I happened to be in Rome on September 11 and watched the Trade Towers go down from my hotel room. In the speeches that the president gave afterwards, of course he said at the conclusion, "God bless the United States of America." One of my European colleagues at the conference I was attending came up to me and said, "How I wish that the prime minister of my country or the president of my country could make such an utterance," but it would be utterly unheard of. You will only hear an American — and perhaps the English, but not the continental Europeans — invoke the deity for the protection of the state. (Remarks at Pew Forum Conference, Chicago, IL, 1/25/02)

Explaining the Constitution's "Establishment" clause

The deeper flaw in the Court's opinion does not lie in its wrong answer to the question whether there was state-induced "peer-pressure" coercion; it lies, rather, in the Court's making violation of the Establishment Clause hinge on such a precious question. The coercion that was a hallmark of historical establishments of religion was coercion of religious orthodoxy and of financial support by force of law and threat of penalty. Typically, attendance at the state church was required; only clergy of the official church could lawfully perform sacraments; and dissenters, if tolerated, faced an array of civil disabilities. Thus, for example, in the colony of Virginia, where the Church of England had been established, ministers were required by law to conform to the doctrine and rites of the Church of England; and all persons were required to attend church and observe the Sabbath, were tithed for the public support of Anglican ministers, and were taxed for the costs of building and repairing churches. The Establishment Clause was adopted to prohibit such an establishment of religion at the federal level.... But there is simply no support for the proposition that the officially sponsored nondenominational invocation and benediction read by Rabbi Gutterman — with no one legally coerced to recite them — violated the Constitution of the United States. To the contrary, they are so characteristically American they could have come from the pen of George Washington or Abraham Lincoln himself. (*Lee v. Weisman*, 505 U.S. 577 [1992])

No "wall of separation"

The founding fathers never used the phrase "separation of church and state." (Remarks to Manhattan Congregation Shearith Israel, New York, NY, 11/22/04)

The *Lemon* test

The Court's three-pronged Lemon *test has been used to determine if there has been an unconstitutional establishment of religion by the state. The three prongs are: 1) secular legislative purpose, 2) principal or primary effect neither enhances nor inhibits religion, 3) does not foster excessive entanglement with religion. While the* Lemon *test may sound nice and neat, it has proven to be a poor and convoluted guide that has been opposed openly by many members of the Court and has created more tensions and conflicts between religion and the government. Antonin Scalia strongly opposes* Lemon. *The following three selections are instructive in understanding his position.*

Lemon Test's motivational witch hunt

While it is possible to discern the objective "purpose" of a statute (*i.e.*, the public good at which its provisions appear to be directed), or even the formal motivation for a statute where that is explicitly set forth (as it was, to no avail, here), discerning the subjective motivation of those enacting the statute is, to be honest, almost always an impossible task. The number of possible motivations, to begin with, is not binary, or indeed even finite. In the present case, for example, a particular legislator need not have voted for the Act either because he wanted to foster religion or because he wanted to improve education. He may have thought the bill would provide jobs for his district, or may have wanted to make amends with a faction of his party he had alienated on another vote, or he may have been a close friend of the bill's sponsor, or he may have been repaying a favor he owed the majority leader, or he may have hoped the Governor would appreciate his vote and make a fundraising appearance for him, or he may have been pressured to vote for a bill he disliked by a wealthy contributor or by a flood of constituent mail, or he may have been seeking favorable publicity, or he may have been reluctant to hurt the feelings of a loyal staff member who worked on the bill, or he may have been settling an old score with a legislator who opposed the bill, or he may have been mad at his wife who opposed the bill, or he may have been intoxicated and utterly *un*motivated when the vote was called, or he may have accidentally voted "yes" instead of "no," or, of course, he may have had (and very likely did have) a combination of some of the above and many other motivations. To look for *the sole purpose* of even a single legislator is probably to look for something that does not exist. (*Edwards v. Aguillard*, 382 U.S. 578, [1987])

Abandoning *Lemon* Test "a good place to start"

In the past we have attempted to justify our embarrassing Establishment Clause jurisprudence on the ground that it "sacrifices clarity and predictability for flexibility." One commentator has aptly characterized this as "a euphemism ... for .. the absence of any principled rationale." I think it time that we sacrifice some "flexibility" for "clarity and predictability." Abandoning *Lemon*'s purpose test — a test which exacerbates the tension between the Free Exercise and Establishment Clauses [and] has no basis in the language or history of the Amendment — would be a good place to start. (*Edwards v. Aguillard*, 382 U.S. 578, [1987])

Lemon Test "ghoul in a late-night horror movie"

As to the Court's invocation of the *Lemon* test: like some ghoul in a late-night horror movie that repeatedly sits up in its grave and shuffles abroad after being repeatedly killed and buried, *Lemon* stalks our Establishment Clause jurisprudence once again, frightening the little children and school attorneys of Center Moriches Union Free School District. Its most recent burial, only last Term, was, to be sure, not fully six feet under: Our decision in *Lee v. Weisman* conspicuously avoided using the supposed "test," but also declined the invitation to repudiate it.

The secret of the *Lemon* test's survival, I think, is that it is so easy to kill. It is there to scare us (and our audience) when we wish it to do so, but we can command it to return to the tomb at will. When we wish to strike down a practice it forbids, we invoke it; when we wish to uphold a practice it forbids, we ignore it entirely. Sometimes, we take a middle course, calling its three prongs "no more than helpful signposts." Such a docile and useful monster is worth keeping around, at least in a somnolent state; one never knows when one might need him.

For my part, I agree with the long list of constitutional scholars who have criticized *Lemon* and bemoaned the strange Establishment Clause geometry of crooked lines and wavering shapes its intermittent use has produced. I will decline to apply *Lemon*. … (*Lamb's Chapel v. Ctr. Moriches Union Free Sch. Dist.*, 508 U.S. 384 [1993])

No requirement of neutrality between religion and non-religion

I believe the single most important thing is the so-called principle of neutrality, which the Court has pronounced, which says that the government, state and federal, must be neutral, not only among various denominations of religion, but must be neutral between religiousness and non-religiousness. That is new, because as recently as the 1940s, in an opinion by, of all people, William O. Douglas, that notorious religious conservative, the Court commented on a released-time program for New York City school students. I was actually in the program, where you'd get Wednesday off if you had a note from your parents and you could go to religious instruction, skip out of school while your classmates who didn't have the notes had to put in another hour-and-a-half or so. It … was challenged in the Court as unconstitutional. The Court upheld it, and writing for the Court, Douglas said we are a religious people whose institutions presuppose a supreme being. When the state accommodates its schedule to the religious needs of its people, it acts in the best of our traditions. Now that was what I think the proper principle of Establishment Clause jurisprudence is. But within 10 years the Court did a flip and said you cannot favor religion over non-religion. The problem with that is that it simply does not comport with our whole constitutional tradition, with so many elements of it: the Thanksgiving proclamations from the beginning, with chaplains in Congress, with chaplains in the armed forces. You don't let people take their philosopher with them, but chaplains. We're favoring religion over non-religion. Tax exemptions for places of worship, there is no way to square that principle with the reality of American constitutional law, yet the Court continues to mouth that principle of neutrality. (Remarks at Pew Forum Conference, Chicago, IL, 1/25/02)

There is something wrong with the principle of neutrality.... [The proper principle] is not neutrality between religiousness and nonreligiousness; it is between denominations of religion. (Remarks to Manhattan Congregation Shearith Israel, New York, NY, 11/22/04)

Indifference to religion not mandated

It suffices to point out that during the summer of 1789, when it was in the process of drafting the First Amendment, Congress enacted the famous Northwest Territory Ordinance of 1789, Article III of which provides, 'Religion, morality, and knowledge, being necessary to good government and the happiness of mankind, schools and the means of education shall forever be encouraged.' Unsurprisingly, then, indifference to 'religion in general' is not what our cases, both old and recent, demand. (*Lamb's Chapel v. Ctr. Moriches Union Free Sch. Dist.*, 508 U.S. 384 [1993])

Government can support "public virtues inculcated by religion"

[I disagree with] the Court's statement that the proposed use of the school's facilities is constitutional because (among other things) it would not signal endorsement of religion in general. What a strange notion, that a Constitution which itself gives a "religion in general" preferential treatment (I refer to the Free Exercise Clause) forbids endorsement of religion in general. The Attorney General of New York not only agrees with that strange notion, he has an explanation for it: "Religious advocacy," he writes, "serves the community only in the eyes of its adherents and yields a benefit only to those who already believe." That was not the view of those who adopted our Constitution, who believed that the public virtues inculcated by religion are a public good. (*Lamb's Chapel v. Ctr. Moriches Union Free Sch. Dist.*, 508 U.S. 384 [1993])

"Psychological coercion" test unwarranted

As its instrument of destruction, the bulldozer of its social engineering, the Court invents a boundless, and boundlessly manipulable, test of psychological coercion.... Today's opinion shows more forcefully than volumes of argumentation why our Nation's protection, that fortress which is our Constitution, cannot possibly rest upon the changeable philosophical predilections of the Justices of this Court, but must have deep foundations in the historic practices of our people. (*Lee v. Weisman*, 505 U.S. 577 [1992])

Constitution does not prohibit public acknowledgment of God

The issue before us today is not the abstract philosophical question whether the alternative of frustrating this desire of a religious majority is to be preferred over the alternative of imposing "psychological coercion," or a feeling of exclusion, upon nonbelievers. Rather, the question is *whether a mandatory choice in favor of the former has been imposed by the United States Constitution.* As the age-old practices of our people show, the answer to that question is not at all in doubt. (*Lee v. Weisman*, 505 U.S. 577 [1992])

Public acknowledgment of God vital to our nation's heritage

From our Nation's origin, prayer has been a prominent part of governmental ceremonies and proclamations. The Declaration of Independence, the document marking our birth as a separate people, "appeal[ed] to the Supreme Judge of the world for the rectitude of our intentions" and avowed "a firm reliance on the protection of divine

Providence." In his first inaugural address, after swearing his oath of office on a Bible, George Washington deliberately made a prayer a part of his first official act as President. (*Lee v. Weisman*, 505 U.S. 577 [1992])

In holding that the Establishment Clause prohibits invocations and benedictions at public-school graduation ceremonies, the Court — with nary a mention that it is doing so — lays waste a tradition that is as old as public-school graduation ceremonies themselves, and that is a component of an even more longstanding American tradition of nonsectarian prayer to God at public celebrations generally. (*Lee v. Weisman*, 505 U.S. 577 [1992])

CHAPTER 6

Defending the Free Exercise of Religion

We need judicial conservatives who will defend the free exercise of religion while opposing the anti-religious trajectory of the courts.

This case is about discrimination against a religious minority....
One need not delve too far into modern popular culture to perceive
a trendy disdain for deep religious conviction.
Justice Antonin Scalia, *Locke v. Davey*, 2004

"I would hold that discriminatory treatment of the [kindergarten student's
Thanksgiving] poster because of its "religious theme" would violate the First
Amendment....The poster was allegedly given discriminatory treatment because of the
viewpoint that it expressed, because it expressed thanks for Jesus, rather than for some
secular thing. This was quintessential viewpoint discrimination."
Samuel Alito, *C.H. v. Olivia*, 2000, dissent.

---

*T*he other side of the coin of the First Amendment's religion protection is the Free Exercise Clause: "Congress shall make no
law...prohibiting the free exercise thereof." As an outgrowth of its
Establishment rulings, the courts have steadily encroached on the free exer-
cise of religion. For example, cases have been brought before the Supreme
Court involving the denial of the use of public facilities to religious groups
and whether certain citizens can be denied state benefits solely on religious
grounds. The right of individuals to speak on matters of faith in public or
to pray at state-sponsored events has also been questioned.

Clearly, there is an anti-religious trajectory in American jurispru-
dence. Antonin Scalia calls such anti-religious rulings "viewpoint discrim-
ination." Such discrimination, specifically banned by the intent of the
First Amendment, is leading quickly toward repression on the basis of reli-
gion. Antonin Scalia opposes such discrimination. In his writings, he has
outlined what we call the Scalia model—a view that will honor the
sacred constitutional right of the free exercise of religion while standing
against the rising tide of anti-religious bigotry in the courts. Samuel Alito's
writings also indicate his opposition to such viewpoint discrimination.
Let's examine the Scalia model and Alito's views. —S.E.

The Scalia Model on Defending the Free Exercise of Religion

"Viewpoint discrimination" explained

From no other group does respondent require the sterility of speech that it demands of petitioners [a religious group]. The Boy Scouts could undoubtedly buttress their exhortations to keep "morally straight" and live "clean" lives by giving reasons why that is a good idea — because parents want and expect it, because it will make the scouts "better" and "more successful" people, because it will emulate such admired past Scouts as former President Gerald Ford. The Club, however, may only discuss morals and character, and cannot give its reasons why they should be fostered — because God wants and expects it, because it will make the Club members "saintly" people, and because it emulates Jesus Christ. The Club may not, in other words, independently discuss the religious premise on which its views are based — that God exists and His assistance is necessary to morality. It may not defend the premise, and it absolutely must not seek to persuade the children that the premise is true. The children must, so to say, take it on faith. This is blatant viewpoint discrimination. Just as calls to character based on patriotism will go unanswered if the listeners do not believe their country is good and just, calls to moral behavior based on God's will are useless if the listeners do not believe that God exists. Effectiveness in presenting a viewpoint rests on the persuasiveness with which the speaker defends his premise — and in respondent's facilities every premise but a religious one may be defended. (*Good News Club et al. v. Milford Central School*, 533 U.S. 98 [2001])

State cannot discriminate benefits based on religion

When the State makes a public benefit generally available, that benefit becomes part of the baseline against which burdens on religion are measured; and when the State withholds that benefit from some individuals solely on the basis of religion, it violates the Free Exercise

Clause no less than if it had imposed a special tax. That is precisely what the State of Washington has done here. It has created a generally available public benefit, whose receipt is conditioned only on academic performance, income, and attendance at an accredited school. It has then carved out a solitary course of study for exclusion: theology. No field of study but religion is singled out for disfavor in this fashion. Davey is not asking for a special benefit to which others are not entitled. He seeks only equal treatment — the right to direct his scholarship to his chosen course of study, a right every other Promise Scholar enjoys. (*Locke v. Davey*, 299 F.3d 748 reversed [2004])

State cannot deny ministers benefits others receive

One can concede the Framers' hostility to funding the clergy specifically, but that says nothing about whether the clergy had to be excluded from benefits the State made available to all. No one would seriously contend, for example, that the Framers would have barred ministers from using public roads on their way to church. (*Locke v. Davey*, 299 F.3d 748 reversed [2004])

Court has discriminated "against a religious minority"

Those singled out for disfavor can be forgiven for suspecting more invidious forces at work. Let there be no doubt: This case is about discrimination against a religious minority. Most citizens of this country identify themselves as professing some religious belief, but the State's policy poses no obstacle to practitioners of only a tepid, civic version of faith. Those the statutory exclusion actually affects–those whose belief in their religion is so strong that they dedicate their study and their lives to its ministry–are a far narrower set. One need not delve too far into modern popular culture to perceive a trendy disdain for deep religious conviction. In an era when the Court is so quick to come to the aid of other disfavored groups, see, *e.g.*, *Romer v. Evans*, 517 U.S. 620, 635 (1996), its indifference in this case, which involves a form of discrimination to which the Constitution actually speaks, is exceptional. (*Locke v. Davey*, 299 F.3d 748 reversed [2004])

Court can't have it both ways

The Court does not dispute that the Free Exercise Clause places some constraints on public benefits programs, but finds none here, based on a principle of "play in the joints." I use the term "principle" loosely, for that is not so much a legal principle as a refusal to apply any principle when faced with competing constitutional directives. There is nothing anomalous about constitutional commands that abut. A municipality hiring public contractors may not discriminate against blacks or in favor of them; it cannot discriminate a little bit each way and then plead "play in the joints" when hauled into court. If the Religion Clauses demand neutrality, we must enforce them, in hard cases as well as easy ones. (*Locke v. Davey*, 299 F.3d 748 reversed [2004])

Voluntary prayer actually builds unity

I must add one final observation: The founders of our Republic knew the fearsome potential of sectarian religious belief to generate civil dissension and civil strife. And they also knew that nothing, absolutely nothing, is so inclined to foster among religious believers of various faiths a toleration — no, an affection — for one another than voluntarily joining in prayer together, to the God whom they all worship and seek. Needless to say, no one should be compelled to do that, but it is a shame to deprive our public culture of the opportunity, and indeed the encouragement, for people to do it voluntarily. The Baptist or Catholic who heard and joined in the simple and inspiring prayers of Rabbi Gutterman on this official and patriotic occasion was inoculated from religious bigotry and prejudice in a manner that can not be replicated. To deprive our society of that important unifying mechanism, in order to spare the nonbeliever what seems to me the minimal inconvenience of standing or even sitting in respectful nonparticipation, is as senseless in policy as it is unsupported in law. (*Lee v. Weisman*, 505 U.S. 577 [1992])

Slippery slope of anti-religious discrimination

Today's holding is limited to training the clergy, but its logic is readily extendible, and there are plenty of directions to go. What next? Will we deny priests and nuns their prescription-drug benefits on the ground that taxpayers' freedom of conscience forbids medicating the clergy at public expense? This may seem fanciful, but recall that France has proposed banning religious attire from schools, invoking interests in secularism no less benign than those the Court embraces today. When the public's freedom of conscience is invoked to justify denial of equal treatment, benevolent motives shade into indifference and ultimately into repression. Having accepted the justification in this case, the Court is less well equipped to fend it off in the future. (*Locke v. Davey*, 299 F.3d 748 reversed [2004])

CHAPTER 7

Evolution and Academic Freedom

*We need judicial conservatives who will oppose the
secular mandate of evolution-only teaching and uphold
academic freedom in our schools.*

*We stand by in silence while a deeply divided Fifth Circuit bars a
school from even suggesting to students that other theories besides
evolution — including, but not limited to, the Biblical theory of
creation — are worthy of their consideration. I dissent.*
Justice Antonin Scalia, *Tangipahoa v. Freiler,* 2000

*"Students have the right to express religious views in class discussion
or in assigned work, provided that their expression falls within
the scope of the discussion or the assignment and provided that
the school's restriction on expression does not satisfy strict scrutiny."*
Samuel Alito, *C.H. v. Olivia,* 2000, dissent

*One of the most interesting and important subsets of the Court's reli-
gion cases involves the teaching of evolution, origin studies, and the
resulting impact on academic freedom. The Court's rulings have supported
the premise that evolution must be taught in public schools while the
"creation science" alternative to evolution may not be taught.
Furthermore, even suggesting that there may be alternatives to evolution
has been frowned upon by the Court.*

*This debate is vital for two reasons. First, it establishes a secular
mandate (beyond a secular purpose) in our jurisprudence. Second, the ban
on alternatives to evolution undermines academic freedom and intellectual pursuit. Antonin Scalia has clearly stated his view that evolution
ought not be enshrined as the sole explanation in government schools for
the origin and development of life. The rise of "intelligent design" as a
rigorous scientific theory means that the Court will likely once again
address this issue of evolution and academic freedom. Given the importance of this issue and the likelihood that nominees like Samuel Alito will
face this on the Court, let's explore the Scalia model on evolution and
academic freedom. —S.E.*

The Scalia Model on Evolution and Academic Freedom

Scopes in reverse: The Court "is the repressive one"

I am astonished by the Court's unprecedented readiness to reach such a conclusion [that the Act in question lacked a secular purpose], which I can only attribute to an intellectual predisposition created by the facts and the legend of *Scopes v. State* — an instinctive reaction that any governmentally imposed requirements bearing upon the teaching of evolution must be a manifestation of Christian fundamentalist repression. In this case, however, it seems to me the Court's position is the repressive one. The people of Louisiana, including those who are Christian fundamentalists, are quite entitled, as a secular matter, to have whatever scientific evidence there may be against evolution presented in their schools, just as Mr. Scopes was entitled to present whatever scientific evidence there was for it. Perhaps what the Louisiana Legislature has done is unconstitutional because there *is* no such evidence, and the scheme they have established will amount to no more than a presentation of the Book of Genesis. But we cannot say that on the evidence before us in this summary judgment context, which includes ample uncontradicted testimony that "creation science" is a body of scientific knowledge rather than revealed belief. *Infinitely less* can we say (or should we say) that the scientific evidence for evolution is so conclusive that no one could be gullible enough to believe that there is any real scientific evidence to the contrary, so that the legislation's stated purpose must be a lie. Yet that illiberal judgment, that *Scopes*-in-reverse, is ultimately the basis on which the Court's facile rejection of the Louisiana Legislature's purpose must rest. (*Edwards v. Aguillard*, 382 U.S. 578, [1987])

Why origin science does not require a "past creator"

Creation science, its proponents insist, no more must explain *whence* life came than evolution must explain whence came the inanimate materials from which it says life evolved. But even if that were not so, to posit a past creator is not to posit the eternal and personal God who is the object of religious veneration. Indeed, it is not even to posit the "*unmoved* mover" hypothesized by Aristotle and other notably nonfundamentalist philosophers. (*Edwards v. Aguillard*, 382 U.S. 578, [1987])

Coinciding with beliefs of religion not basis for invalidation

We will not presume that a law's purpose is to advance religion merely because it "happens to coincide or harmonize with the tenets of some or all religions," or because it benefits religion, even substantially. We have, for example, turned back Establishment Clause challenges to restrictions on abortion funding, and to Sunday closing laws, despite the fact that both "agre[e] with the dictates of [some] Judaeo-Christian religions...." On many past occasions we have had no difficulty finding a secular purpose for governmental action far more likely to advance religion than the Balanced Treatment Act. Thus, the fact that creation science coincides with the beliefs of certain religions, a fact upon which the majority relies heavily, does not itself justify invalidation of the Act. (*Edwards v. Aguillard*, 382 U.S. 578, [1987])

Individuals can act on religious convictions

Our cases in no way imply that the Establishment Clause forbids legislators merely to act upon their religious convictions. We surely would not strike down a law providing money to feed the hungry or shelter the homeless if it could be demonstrated that, but for the religious beliefs of the legislators, the funds would not have been approved. Also, political activism by the religiously motivated is part of our heritage. Notwithstanding the majority's implication to the contrary, we do not presume that the sole purpose of a law is to advance religion merely because it was supported strongly by organized religions or by adherents of particular faiths. To do so would deprive religious men and women of their right to participate in the political process. Today's religious activism may give us the Balanced Treatment Act, but yesterday's resulted in the abolition of slavery, and tomorrow's may bring relief for famine victims. (*Edwards v. Aguillard,* 382 U.S. 578, [1987])

Balanced evolution teaching may be required by Free Exercise Clause

We have held that intentional governmental advancement of religion is sometimes required by the Free Exercise Clause. For example, we held that in some circumstances States must accommodate the beliefs of religious citizens by exempting them from generally applicable regulations. We have not yet come close to reconciling *Lemon* and our Free Exercise cases, and typically we do not really try. It is clear, however, that members of the Louisiana Legislature were not impermissibly motivated for purposes of the *Lemon* test if they believed that approval of the Balanced Treatment Act was *required* by the Free Exercise Clause. (*Edwards v. Aguillard,* 382 U.S. 578, [1987])

Objective origins teaching in pursuit of academic freedom

Had the Court devoted to this central question of the meaning of the legislatively expressed purpose a small fraction of the research into legislative history that produced its quotations of religiously motivated statements by individual legislators, it would have discerned quite readily what "academic freedom" meant: *students'* freedom from *indoctrination.* The legislature wanted to ensure that students would be free to decide for themselves how life began, based upon a fair and balanced presentation of the scientific evidence — that is, to protect "the right of each [student] voluntarily to determine what to believe (and what not to believe) free of any coercive pressures from the State." The legislature did not care *whether* the topic of origins was taught; it simply wished to ensure that *when* the topic was taught, students would receive "all of the evidence." (*Edwards v. Aguillard,* 382 U.S. 578, [1987])

State should act in this arena to prevent hostility to religion

First, since we have consistently described the Establishment Clause as forbidding not only state action motivated by the desire to *advance* religion, but also that intended to "disapprove," "inhibit," or evince "hostility" toward religion; and since we have said that governmental "neutrality" toward religion is the preeminent goal of the First Amendment; a State which discovers that its employees are inhibiting religion must take steps to prevent them from doing so, even though its purpose would clearly be to advance religion. Thus, if the Louisiana Legislature sincerely believed that the State's science teachers were being hostile to religion, our cases indicate that it could act to eliminate that hostility without running afoul of *Lemon's* purpose test. (*Edwards v. Aguillard,* 382 U.S. 578, [1987])

"No realistic danger" in evolution disclaimer

The only allusion to religion in the entire disclaimer is a reference to the "Biblical version of Creation," mentioned as an illustrative *example* — surely the most obvious example — of a "concept" that the teaching of evolution was "not intended to influence or dissuade." The disclaimer does not refer again to the "Biblical version of Creation," much less provide any elaboration as to what that theory entails; instead, it merely reaffirms that "it is the basic right and privilege of each student to form his/her own opinion or maintain beliefs taught by parents on this very important matter of the origin of life and matter," and neutrally encourages students "closely [to] examine *each* alternative" before forming an opinion. (*Tangipahoa Parish v. Freiler,* No. 99-1625, Cert. Denied, [June 19, 2000])

In view of the fact that the disclaimer merely reminds students of their right to form their own beliefs on the subject, or to maintain beliefs taught by their parents — not to mention the fact that the theory of evolution is the only theory actually taught in the lesson that follows the disclaimer — there is "no realistic danger that the community would think that the [School Board] was endorsing religion or any particular creed, and any benefit to religion or to the Church would have been no more than incidental." (*Tangipahoa Parish v. Freiler,* No. 99-1625, Cert. Denied, [June 19, 2000])

Establishment claim "simply absurd"

To think that this reference to (and plainly not endorsement of) a reality of religious literature — and this use of an example that is not a contrived one, but to the contrary the example most likely to come into play — somehow converts the otherwise innocuous disclaimer into an establishment of religion is quite simply absurd. (*Tangipahoa Parish v. Freiler,* No. 99-1625, Cert. Denied, [June 19, 2000])

Court pushes "legend of the Monkey Trial one step further"

In *Epperson v. Arkansas,* we invalidated a statute that forbade the teaching of evolution in public schools; in *Edwards v. Aguillard,* we invalidated a statute that required the teaching of creationism whenever evolution was also taught; today we permit a Court of Appeals to push the much beloved secular legend of the Monkey Trial one step further. We stand by in silence while a deeply divided Fifth Circuit bars a school district from even suggesting to students that other theories besides evolution — including, but not limited to, the Biblical theory of creation — are worthy of their consideration. I dissent. (*Tangipahoa Parish v. Freiler,* No. 99-1625, Cert. Denied, [June 19, 2000])

CHAPTER 8

Restoring Order on Abortion

*A judicial conservative will work to return
the abortion issue to the states and the people.*

As I made clear in my remarks, I will strike down Roe v. Wade, *but I will also strike down a law that is the opposite of* Roe v. Wade. *You know, both sides in that debate want the Supreme Court to decide the matter for them. One wants no state to be able to prohibit abortion and the other one wants every state to have to prohibit abortion, and they're both wrong, not because of my religious views but because that's how I read the Constitution.*

Justice Antonin Scalia, January 25, 2002

"The Pennsylvania legislature could have rationally believed that some married women are initially inclined to obtain an abortion without their husbands' knowledge because of perceived problems — such as economic constraints, future plans, or the husbands' previously expressed opposition — that may be obviated by discussion prior to the abortion."

Samuel Alito, Planned Parenthood v. Casey, 1991

***

O *ne of the most important debates in our culture over the past 50 years involves abortion. In the 1973 case* Roe v. Wade, *the Supreme Court divined that a fundamental right to an abortion existed within the "penumbras" of the Constitution's guarantee of a right to privacy and personal liberty. In essence, the Court created a right not found in the Constitution, applied that right to the abortion issue, and then invalidated the laws of all 50 states regarding abortion. As a result, abortion is not only legal at any point in pregnancy, it is viewed by the courts as a fundamental right guaranteed by the Constitution.*

Justice Scalia has consistently argued that a right to abortion does not exist within the Constitution. His public statements and opinions clearly state his position: Regardless of his or anyone's personal position on abortion, a judicial conservative in the Scalia model would hold that this is not an issue the courts should decide. Let's explore the Scalia model on abortion, as well as Samuel Alito's views on this important constitutional issue. And let the public debate begin again. —S.E.

The Scalia Model on Restoring Order on Abortion

No "right" to abortion

I do not believe — and no one believed for 200 years — that the Constitution contains a right to abortion. (Remarks at Pew Forum Conference, Chicago, IL, 1/25/02)

It's plain that the right to an abortion was not thought to exist in 1791 or at the time that post-Civil War amendments were adopted; absolutely plain. There were laws against them in all the states. (Remarks at the Catholic University of America, Washington, DC, 10/18/96)

"My difficulty with *Roe*"

Capital cases are much different from the other life-and-death issues that my Court sometimes faces: abortion, for example, or legalized suicide. There it is not the state (of which I am in a sense the last instrument) that is decreeing death, but rather private individuals whom the state has decided not to restrain. One may argue (as many do) that the society has a moral obligation to restrain. That moral obligation may weigh heavily upon the voter, and upon the legislator who enacts the laws; but a judge, I think, bears no moral guilt for the laws society has failed to enact. Thus, my difficulty with *Roe v. Wade* is a legal rather than a moral one: I do not believe (and, for two hundred years, no one believed) that the Constitution contains a right to abortion. (Antonin Scalia, "God's Justice, Not Ours," *First Things 123*, May 2002)

"I will strike down *Roe v. Wade*"

As I made clear in my remarks, I will strike down *Roe v. Wade*, but I will also strike down a law that is the opposite of *Roe v. Wade*. You know, both sides in that debate want the Supreme Court to decide the matter for them. One wants no state to be able to prohibit abortion and the other one wants every state to have to prohibit abortion, and they're both wrong, not because of my religious views but because that's how I read the Constitution. It says nothing on the subject, whatever my religious views on the subject are, and I have religious views on the subject. But they have nothing whatever to do with my job. (Remarks at Pew Forum Conference, Chicago, IL, 1/25/02)

Abortion not a "liberty" right

That is, quite simply, the issue in this case: not whether the power of a woman to abort her unborn child is a "liberty" in the absolute sense; or even whether it is a liberty of great importance to many women. Of course it is both. The issue is whether it is a liberty protected by the Constitution of the United States. I am sure it is not. I reach that conclusion not because of anything so exalted as my views concerning the "concept of existence, of meaning, of the universe, and of the mystery of human life." Rather, I reach it for the same reason I reach the conclusion that bigamy is not constitutionally protected — because of two simple facts: (1) the Constitution says absolutely nothing about it, and (2) the longstanding traditions of American society have permitted it to be legally proscribed. (*Planned Parenthood v. Casey*, 505 U.S. 833 [1992])

The emptiness of the "reasoned judgment" that produced *Roe* is displayed in plain view by the fact that, after more than 19 years of effort by some of the brightest (and most determined) legal minds in the country, after more than 10 cases upholding abortion rights in this Court, and after dozens upon dozens of amicus briefs submitted in this and other cases, the best the Court can do to explain how it is that the word "liberty" must be thought to include the right to destroy human fetuses is to rattle off a collection of adjectives that simply decorate a value judgment and conceal a political choice. The right to abort, we are told, inheres in "liberty" because it is among "a person's most basic decisions;" it involves a "most intimate and personal choic[e];" it is "central to personal dignity and autonomy;" it "originate[s] within the zone of conscience and belief;" it is "too intimate and personal" for state interference; it reflects "intimate views" of a "deep, personal character;" it involves "intimate relationships," and notions of "personal autonomy and bodily integrity;" and it concerns a particularly "important decisio[n]." But it is obvious to anyone applying "reasoned judgment" that the same adjectives can be applied to many forms of conduct that this Court (including one of the Justices in today's majority) has held are not entitled to constitutional protection — because, like abortion, they are forms of conduct that have long been criminalized in American society. Those adjectives might be applied, for example, to homosexual sodomy, polygamy, adult incest, and suicide, all of which are equally "intimate" and "deep[ly] personal" decisions involving "personal autonomy and bodily integrity," and all of which can constitutionally be proscribed because it is our unquestionable constitutional tradition that they are proscribable. It is not reasoned judgment that supports the Court's decision; only personal predilection. (*Planned Parenthood v. Casey*, 505 U.S. 833 [1992])

Abortion should be for political debate

It is no more realistic for us in this case than it was for him in that to think that an issue of the sort they both involved — an issue involving life and death, freedom and subjugation — can be "speedily and finally settled" by the Supreme Court, as President James Buchanan, in his inaugural address, said the issue of slavery in the territories would be. Quite to the contrary, by foreclosing all democratic outlet for the deep passions this issue arouses, by banishing the issue from the political forum that gives all participants, even the losers, the satisfaction of a fair hearing and an honest fight, by continuing the imposition of a rigid national rule instead of allowing for regional differences, the Court merely prolongs and intensifies the anguish. We should get out of this area, where we have no right to be, and where we do neither ourselves nor the country any good by remaining. (*Planned Parenthood v. Casey*, 505 U.S. 833 [1992])

Alone sufficient to justify a broad holding is the fact that our retaining control, through *Roe*, of what I believe to be, and many of our citizens recognize to be, a political issue, continuously distorts the public perception of the role of this Court. We can now look forward to at least another Term with carts full of mail from the public, and streets full of demonstrators, urging us - their unelected and life-tenured judges who have been awarded those extraordinary, undemocratic characteristics precisely in order that we might follow the law despite the popular will - to follow the popular will. Indeed, I expect we can look forward to even more of that than before, given our indecisive decision today. ... It thus appears that the mansion of constitutionalized abortion law, constructed overnight in *Roe v. Wade*, must be disassembled doorjamb by doorjamb, and never entirely brought down, no matter how wrong it may be. (*Webster v. Reproductive Health Services*, 492 U.S. 490 [1989])

The outcome of today's case will doubtless be heralded as a triumph of judicial statesmanship. It is not that, unless it is statesman-like needlessly to prolong this Court's self-awarded sovereignty over a field where it has little proper business since the answers to most of the cruel questions posed are political and not juridical — a sovereignty which therefore quite properly, but to the great damage of the Court, makes it the object of the sort of organized public pressure that political institutions in a democracy ought to receive. (*Webster v. Reproductive Health Services*, 492 U.S. 490 [1989])

Not about personal opinions

Does this statute, let's say it's parental notification or who knows what, whatever. Does this place an undue burden on a woman's right to an abortion? I don't know, what do you think? Do you think it places an undue burden? How about you? Think it's an undue burden? How many think it places an undue burden? That's five. This is not law. This is not law but policy-making. (Remarks at U.S. Association of Constitutional Law Discussion, Washington, DC, 1/13/05)

If a state were to permit abortion on demand, I would — and could in good conscience — vote against an attempt to invalidate that law for the same reason that I vote against the invalidation of laws that forbid abortion on demand: because the Constitution gives the federal government (and hence me) no power over the matter. (Antonin Scalia, "God's Justice, Not Ours," *First Things 123*, May 2002)

Partial-Birth Abortion

In 2000, the Supreme Court in Stenberg v. Carhart *struck down a Nebraska state law banning the brutal late-term abortion procedure known as dilation and extraction, commonly referred to as partial-birth abortion. In a partial-birth abortion procedure, the unborn child is partially delivered feet first, leaving the head as the only part of the body remaining in the birth canal. The abortionist punctures the base of the unborn child's skull and suctions out the brain matter, killing the child. This process collapses the empty skull and eases the removal of the dead child from the birth canal. Justice Scalia argues that it is utterly absurd to suggest the Constitution protects this brutal form of abortion as a fundamental right. It is the right of the people through their elected representatives to decide whether to outlaw this horrific practice. —S.E.*

I am optimistic enough to believe that, one day, *Stenberg v. Carhart* will be assigned its rightful place in the history of this Court's jurisprudence beside *Korematsu* and *Dred Scott*. The method of killing a human child — one cannot even accurately say an entirely unborn human child — proscribed by this statute is so horrible that the most clinical description of it evokes a shudder of revulsion. And the Court must know (as most state legislatures banning this procedure have concluded) that demanding a "health exception"–which requires the abortionist to assure himself that, in his expert medical judgment, this method is, in the case at hand, marginally safer than others (how can one prove the contrary beyond a reasonable doubt?)–is to give live-birth abortion free rein. The notion that the Constitution of the United States, designed, among other things, "to establish Justice, insure domestic Tranquility ... and secure the Blessings of Liberty to ourselves and our Posterity," prohibits the States from simply banning this visibly brutal means of eliminating our half-born posterity is quite simply absurd. (*Stenberg v. Carhart*, 530 U.S. 914 [2000])

Today's decision, that the Constitution of the United States prevents the prohibition of a horrible mode of abortion, will be greeted by a firestorm of criticism — as well it should. I cannot understand why those who acknowledge that, in the opening words of Justice O'Connor's concurrence, "[t]he issue of abortion is one of the most contentious and controversial in contemporary American society," persist in the belief that this Court, armed with neither constitutional text nor accepted tradition, can resolve that contention and controversy rather than be consumed by it. If only for the sake of its own preservation, the Court should return this matter to the people — where the Constitution, by its silence on the subject, left it — and let them decide, State by State, whether this practice should be allowed. (*Stenberg v. Carhart*, 530 U.S. 914 [2000])

CHAPTER 9

Free Speech, Even on Abortion

*How a judicial conservative will help undo the
constraint on pro-life free speech and work
to restore free speech for all.*

None of these remarkable conclusions should come as a surprise. What is before us, after all, is a speech regulation directed against the opponents of abortion.... Having deprived abortion opponents of the political right to persuade the electorate that abortion should be restricted by law, the Court today continues and expands its assault upon their individual right to persuade women contemplating abortion that what they are doing is wrong.
Justice Antonin Scalia, *Hill v. Colorado*, 2000

"I am particularly proud of my contributions in recent cases in which the government has argued that...the Constitution does not protect a right to an abortion."
Samuel Alito, 1985

*S*ince *the Supreme Court legalized abortion on-demand with its 1973 ruling in* Roe v. Wade, *pro-life activists have worked tirelessly to bring attention to the plight of the unborn child. Every year on the anniversary of* Roe v. Wade, *thousands of Americans descend on Washington, D.C., for the March for Life, an event designed to remind the government that Americans support the right to life from conception. Thousands of pro-lifers stand outside abortion clinics across the country, praying and trying to educate women about the facts of abortion.*

Unfortunately, the Supreme Court has ruled against the free speech rights of citizens when discussing the abortion issue. Justice Scalia has consistently argued against such content-based ban on speech, which the Court eagerly applies to the abortion issue but will not allow on other topics. This is the Scalia model for a judicial conservative who desires to uphold the Constitution. Let's explore more closely how this model will eliminate this double standard and protect all Americans from content-based prohibitions on speech. —S.E.

The Scalia Model on Free Speech, Even on Abortion

Content-based free speech restriction

Colorado's statute makes it a criminal act knowingly to approach within 8 feet of another person on the public way or sidewalk area within 100 feet of the entrance door of a health care facility for the purpose of passing a leaflet to, displaying a sign to, or engaging in oral protest, education, or counseling with such person. Whatever may be said about the restrictions on the other types of expressive activity, the regulation as it applies to oral communications is obviously and undeniably content-based. A speaker wishing to approach another for the purpose of communicating any message except one of protest, education, or counseling may do so without first securing the other's consent. Whether a speaker must obtain permission before approaching within eight feet–and whether he will be sent to prison for failing to do so–depends entirely on what he intends to say when he gets there. I have no doubt that this regulation would be deemed content-based in an instant if the case before us involved antiwar protesters, or union members seeking to "educate" the public about the reasons for their strike. "[I]t is," we would say, "the content of the speech that determines whether it is within or without the statute's blunt prohibition." But the jurisprudence of this Court has a way of changing when abortion is involved. (*Hill v. Colorado*, 530 U.S. 703 [2000])

Court "expands its assault" on pro-life rights

None of these remarkable conclusions should come as a surprise. What is before us, after all, is a speech regulation directed against the opponents of abortion. ... Having deprived abortion opponents of the political right to persuade the electorate that abortion should be restricted by law, the Court today continues and expands its assault upon their individual right to persuade women contemplating abortion that what they are doing is wrong. (*Hill v. Colorado*, 530 U.S. 703 [2000])

A "distortion" of the First Amendment

There is apparently no end to the distortion of our First Amendment law that the Court is willing to endure in order to sustain this restriction upon the free speech of abortion opponents. ... Nothing stands in the way of that solution to the narrow-tailoring problem — except, of course, its utter absurdity, which is no obstacle in abortion cases. (*Hill v. Colorado*, 530 U.S. 703 [2000])

Eliminating "forum of last resort"

The public forum involved here–the public spaces outside of health care facilities–has become, by necessity and by virtue of this Court's decisions, a forum of last resort for those who oppose abortion. The possibility of limiting abortion by legislative means–even abortion of a live-and-kicking child that is almost entirely out of the womb–has been rendered impossible by our decisions from *Roe v. Wade* to *Stenberg v. Carhart*. For those who share an abiding moral or religious conviction (or, for that matter, simply a biological appreciation) that abortion is the taking of a human life, there is no option but to persuade women, one by one, not to make that choice. And as a general matter, the most effective place, if not the only place, where that persuasion can occur, is outside the entrances to abortion facilities. By upholding these restrictions on speech in this place the Court ratifies the State's attempt to make even that task an impossible one. ... [T]hose who would accomplish their moral and religious objectives by peaceful and civil means, by trying to persuade individual women of the rightness of their cause, will be deterred; and that is not a good thing in a democracy. (*Hill v. Colorado*, 530 U.S. 703 [2000])

A court-imposed "pro-abortion novelty"

Does the deck seem stacked? You bet. As I have suggested throughout this opinion, today's decision is not an isolated distortion of our traditional constitutional principles, but is one of many aggressively proabortion novelties announced by the Court in recent years. Today's distortions, however, are particularly blatant. Restrictive views of the First Amendment that have been in dissent since the 1930's suddenly find themselves in the majority. "Uninhibited, robust, and wide open" debate is replaced by the power of the state to protect an unheard-of "right to be let alone" on the public streets. (*Hill v. Colorado*, 530 U.S. 703 [2000])

Court responding to offense of pro-life movement

But whether it would "subvert the Court's legitimacy" or not, the notion that we would decide a case differently from the way we otherwise would have in order to show that we can stand firm against public disapproval is frightening. It is a bad enough idea, even in the head of someone like me, who believes that the text of the Constitution, and our traditions, say what they say and there is no fiddling with them. But when it is in the mind of a Court that believes the Constitution has an evolving meaning ... then the notion that the Court must adhere to a decision for as long as the decision faces "great opposition" and the Court is "under fire" acquires a character of almost czarist arrogance. We are offended by these marchers who descend upon us, every year on the anniversary of *Roe*, to protest our saying that the Constitution requires what our society has never thought the Constitution requires. These people who refuse to be "tested by following" must be taught a lesson. We have no Cossacks, but at least we can stubbornly refuse to abandon an erroneous opinion that we might otherwise change — to show how little they intimidate us. (*Planned Parenthood v. Casey*, 505 U.S. 833 [1992])

CHAPTER 10

Defending Political Free Speech

*A judicial conservative must defend the
First Amendment right of citizens
to criticize the government.*

We are governed by Congress, and this legislation prohibits the criticism
of Members of Congress by those entities most capable of giving such
criticism loud voice: national political parties and corporations, both of
the commercial and the not-for-profit sort. It forbids pre-election criticism
of incumbents by corporations, even not-for profit corporations, by use of
their general funds; and forbids national-party use of "soft" money to
fund "issue ads" that incumbents find so offensive.
Justice Antonin Scalia, *McConnell v. FEC*, 2003

"If government were free to suppress disfavored speech by preventing
potential speakers from being paid, there would not be much
left of the First Amendment. Imposing a financial burden on a
speaker based on the content of the speaker's expression is a
content-based restriction of expression and must be analyzed as such."
Samuel Alito, *Pitt News v. Pappert*, 2004.

---

*I*n *2002, Congress passed and the president signed the McCain-
Feingold "Bipartisan Campaign Reform Act." The bill prohibits,
among other things, independent issue advertisements 30 days before a
primary or 60 days before a general election. For example, the National
Right to Life Committee was prohibited in the 2004 election from airing
an ad stating the facts about John Kerry's voting record on abortion.*

*Despite its good intentions, this law is a blatant restriction of free
speech that threatens speech in a host of arenas including the Internet.
Interestingly, while the Court has seen fit to expand speech rights in some
areas (virtual child pornography, sexual television programming) it will-
ingly goes along with the legislature to restrict political speech—what
Antonin Scalia calls the "heart of what the First Amendment is meant to
protect." As a Justice, Scalia has upheld the First Amendment's ban on
abridgements of the "freedom of speech" and as set out an excellent model
for judicial conservatives who seek to honor the Constitution. Nominees*

like Samuel Alito face the challenge of upholding the Scalia model that defends our right to criticize our government.—S.E.

The Scalia Model on Defending Political Free Speech

"Sad day for the freedom of speech"

This is a sad day for the freedom of speech. Who could have imagined that the same Court which, within the past four years, has sternly disapproved of restrictions upon such inconsequential forms of expression as virtual child pornography, tobacco advertising, dissemination of illegally intercepted communications, and sexually explicit cable programming, would smile with favor upon a law that cuts to the heart of what the First Amendment is meant to protect: the right to criticize the government. For that is what the most offensive provisions of this legislation are all about. (*McConnell v. FEC*, 251 F. Supp. 2d 176, 251 F. Supp. 2d 948, affirmed in part and reversed in part [2003])

Frustrates "fundamental purpose of the First Amendment"

Our traditional view was correct, and today's cavalier attitude toward regulating the financing of speech ... frustrates the fundamental purpose of the First Amendment. (*McConnell v. FEC*, 251 F. Supp. 2d 176, 251 F. Supp. 2d 948, affirmed in part and reversed in part [2003])

Prohibits criticism of Congress

We are governed by Congress, and this legislation prohibits the criticism of Members of Congress by those entities most capable of giving such criticism loud voice: national political parties and corporations, both of the commercial and the not-for-profit sort. It forbids pre-election criticism of incumbents by corporations, even not-for-profit corporations, by use of their general funds; and forbids national-party use of "soft" money to fund "issue ads" that incumbents find so offensive. (*McConnell v. FEC*, 251 F. Supp. 2d 176, 251 F. Supp. 2d 948, affirmed in part and reversed in part [2003])

McCain-Feingold favors incumbents

To be sure, the legislation is evenhanded: It similarly prohibits criticism of the candidates who oppose Members of Congress in their reelection bids. But as everyone knows, this is an area in which evenhandedness is not fairness. If all electioneering were evenhandedly prohibited, incumbents would have an enormous advantage. Likewise, if incumbents and challengers are limited to the same quantity of electioneering, incumbents are favored. In other words, any restriction upon a type of campaign speech that is equally available to challengers and incumbents tends to favor incumbents. (*McConnell v. FEC*, 251 F. Supp. 2d 176, 251 F. Supp. 2d 948, affirmed in part and reversed in part [2003])

Beyond that, however, the present legislation targets for prohibition certain categories of campaign speech that are particularly harmful to incumbents. Is it accidental, do you think, that incumbents raise about three times as much "hard money" — the sort of funding generally not restricted by this legislation — as do their challengers? Or that lobbyists (who seek the favor of incumbents) give 92 percent of their money in "hard" contributions? Is it an oversight, do you suppose, that the so-called "millionaire provisions" raise the contribution limit for a candidate running against an individual who devotes to the campaign (as challengers often do) great personal wealth, but do not raise the limit for a candidate running against an individual who devotes to the campaign (as incumbents often do) a massive election "war chest"? And is it mere happenstance, do you estimate, that national-party funding, which is severely limited by the Act, is more likely to assist cash-strapped challengers than flush-with-hard-money incumbents? Was it unintended, by any chance, that incumbents are free personally to receive some soft money and even to solicit it for other organizations, while national parties are not? (*McConnell v. FEC*, 251 F. Supp. 2d 176, 251 F. Supp. 2d 948, affirmed in part and reversed in part [2003])

Opportunity for government control

In any economy operated on even the most rudimentary principles of division of labor, effective public communication requires the speaker to make use of the services of others. An author may write a novel, but he will seldom publish and distribute it himself. A freelance reporter may write a story, but he will rarely edit, print, and deliver it to subscribers. To a government bent on suppressing speech, this mode of organization presents opportunities: Control any cog in the machine, and you can halt the whole apparatus. … Division of labor requires a means of mediating exchange, and in a commercial society, that means is supplied by money. (*McConnell v. FEC*, 251 F. Supp. 2d 176, 251 F. Supp. 2d 948, affirmed in part and reversed in part [2003])

CHAPTER 11

Death Not a Right

A judicial conservative rejects the "right to die" as a constitutional imperative and thereby upholds the implicit life principle in our society.

The point at which the means necessary to preserve it become "extraordinary" or "inappropriate," are neither set forth in the Constitution nor known to the nine Justices of this Court any better than they are known to nine people picked at random from the Kansas City telephone directory.

Justice Antonin Scalia, *Cruzan v. Director, Missouri Department of Health,* 1990

"This is a problem of weighing important, but nevertheless extra-constitutional, values. It is a problem of balancing, of picking and choosing, of drawing fine lines. Legislative and rulemaking bodies are well-equipped for this task; courts are not."

Samuel Alito, 1986

―――――――――――――――――――――――――――――――――

*W*ith the advances in medical technology and the increasing ability to keep the body alive longer and longer, our society is heading full-steam toward a political and legal showdown on issues related to human death. At its particulars, this is an extremely complex issue, as demonstrated by the national debate surrounding the late Terri Schiavo to cite just one example.*

It is now evident that the courts are heading in the direction of creating a constitutional "right to die," similar to the right to abortion, as a liberty and privacy right. Antonin Scalia rightly sees no such "right to die" in the penumbras of the Constitution. Judgers and justices in the Scalia model will work to ensure that no such right is created while minizing federal court intervention in this realm, thereby upholding the implicit life principle in our society. This could prove to be among the most significant issues nominees like Samuel Alito will face. Let's explore the model and apply Alito's record. —S.E.

The Scalia Model on Death Not a Right

"Right to die" not in Constitution

Bear in mind that I don't make up new constitutional rules. I don't sit back and say should there be a right to die. You know, it's not really there in the Constitution, but you know, we have an evolving Constitution and maybe it ought to be there. Now, if that's the kind of judge I was, I would certainly think that my ethical and moral and religious views would have a lot to do with my decisions. But I am not that kind of a judge. I look at a text. I take my best shot at getting the fairest meaning of that text, and where it is a constitutional text, understanding what it meant at the time it was adopted. (Remarks at Pew Forum Conference, Chicago, IL, 1/25/02)

Starving oneself to death is no different from putting a gun to one's temple as far as the common-law definition of suicide is concerned; the cause of death in both cases is the suicide's conscious decision to "pu[t] an end to his own existence." (*Cruzan v. Director, Missouri Department of Health*, 497 U.S. 261 [1990])

Not a "federal constitutional imperative"

The various opinions in this case portray quite clearly the difficult, indeed agonizing, questions that are presented by the constantly increasing power of science to keep the human body alive for longer than any reasonable person would want to inhabit it. The States have begun to grapple with these problems through legislation. I am concerned, from the tenor of today's opinions, that we are poised to confuse that enterprise as successfully as we have confused the enterprise of legislating concerning abortion, requiring it to be conducted against a background of federal constitutional imperatives that are unknown because they are being newly crafted from Term to Term. That would be a great misfortune. (*Cruzan v. Director, Missouri Department of Health*, 497 U.S. 261 [1990])

Courts have "no business in this field"

While I agree with the Court's analysis today, and therefore join in its opinion, I would have preferred that we announce, clearly and promptly, that the federal courts have no business in this field; that American law has always accorded the State the power to prevent, by force if necessary, suicide, including suicide by refusing to take appropriate measures necessary to preserve one's life; that the point at which life becomes "worthless," and the point at which the means necessary to preserve it become "extraordinary" or "inappropriate," are neither set forth in the Constitution nor known to the nine Justices of this Court any better than they are known to nine people picked at random from the Kansas City telephone directory; and hence, that even when it is demonstrated by clear and convincing evidence that a patient no longer wishes certain measures to be taken to preserve her life, it is up to the citizens of Missouri to decide, through their elected representatives, whether that wish will be honored. It is quite impossible (because the Constitution says nothing about the matter) that those citizens will decide upon a line less lawful than the one we would choose; and it is unlikely (because we know no more about "life-and-death" than they do) that they will decide upon a line less reasonable. (*Cruzan v. Director, Missouri Department of Health*, 497 U.S. 261 [1990])

Courts can't protect us from everything

Are there, then, no reasonable and humane limits that ought not to be exceeded in requiring an individual to preserve his own life? There obviously are, but they are not set forth in the Due Process Clause. What assures us that those limits will not be exceeded is the same constitutional guarantee that is the source of most of our protection; what protects us, for example, from being assessed a tax of 100% of our income above the subsistence level, from being forbidden to drive cars, or from being required to send our children to school for 10 hours a day, none of which horrible; is categorically prohibited by the

Constitution. Our salvation is the Equal Protection Clause, which requires the democratic majority to accept for themselves and their loved ones what they impose on you and me. This Court need not, and has no authority to, inject itself into every field of human activity where irrationality and oppression may theoretically occur, and if it tries to do so it will destroy itself. (*Cruzan v. Director, Missouri Department of Health*, 497 U.S. 261 [1990])

CHAPTER 12

Death Penalty with Due Process

A judicial conservative must uphold "due process" in death penalty and other life, liberty, and property cases.

For me, the constitutionality of the death penalty is not a difficult,
soul-wrenching question. It was clearly permitted
when the Eighth Amendment was adopted —
not merely for murder, by the way, but for all felonies.
Justice Antonin Scalia, January 25, 2002

"It appears to us that Rompilla is now arguing that his trial counsel were
constitutionally derelict in failing to take all the steps that might have been pursued by
the most resourceful defense attorneys with bountiful investigative support. But while we
may hope for the day when every criminal defendant receives that level of representation,
that is more than the Sixth Amendment demands."
Samuel Alito, *Rompilla v. Horn*, 2004.

---

*F*ew may realize the death penalty is mentioned in the U.S.
Constitution. The 14th Amendment reads, "[N]or shall any state
deprive any person of life, liberty, or property, without due process of law."
This clearly implies that, under the Constitution, the state does have the
ability to take the life of a criminal who has been appropriately tried and
convicted as long as "due process" is maintained.

However, the Supreme Court in recent years has restricted the death
penalty under the false banner of the Eighth Amendment's prohibition of
"cruel and unusual" punishments. Justice Scalia argues that, while states
are free to prohibit the death penalty, the Constitution does not prohibit
the death penalty under the Eighth Amendment. Capital punishment was
not "cruel and unusual" when the Constitution was drafted and so consti-
tutionally it remains that way today. A judicial conservative would not
approach the bench or a case with a desire to advance a death penalty
agenda. To the contrary, a judicial conservative recognizes the validity of
deprivations of life, liberty and property as long as constitutional due
process is present. Samuel Alito and other nominees to the Court face the
challenge of resisting a politically correct agenda in favor of upholding the

Constitutional due process provision. For background, let's explore the Scalia model. —S.E.

The Scalia Model on Death Penalty with Due Process

Constitutionality of death penalty "not difficult"

[T]he Constitution that I interpret and apply is not living, but dead; or as I prefer to call it, enduring. It means today not what current society, much less the Court, thinks it ought to mean, but what it meant when it was adopted. For me, therefore, the constitutionality of the death penalty is not a difficult, soul-wrenching question. It was clearly permitted when the Eighth Amendment was adopted — not merely for murder, by the way, but for all felonies, including, for example, horse thieving, as anyone can verify by watching a western movie. And so it is clearly permitted today as far as the Constitution is concerned. (Remarks at Pew Forum Conference, Chicago, IL, 1/25/02)

Not cruel and unusual punishment

[T]he legal issue for me as a judge is whether the death penalty, as it is administered, violates the Eighth Amendment. Does it constitute cruel and unusual punishment? The answer is no. It does not even if you don't allow mitigating evidence in. I mean, my court made up that requirement. That was never a requirement when the Eighth Amendment was adopted. Now maybe it's a good idea. So pass a statute, or if you want to make every state do that, adopt a constitutional amendment. But I don't think my Court is authorized to say, oh, it would be a good idea to have every jury be able to consider mitigating evidence and grant mercy. And, oh, it would be a good idea not to have mandatory death penalties. (Remarks at Pew Forum Conference, Chicago, IL, 1/25/02)

Death Penalty "not immoral"

That is not to say I favor the death penalty (I am judicially and judiciously neutral on that point); it is only to say that I do not find the death penalty immoral. (Remarks at Pew Forum Conference, Chicago, IL, 1/25/02)

"Evolving standards" hypothesis untenable

Of course, the real force driving today's decision is not the actions of four state legislatures, but the Court's "own judgment" that murderers younger than 18 can never be as morally culpable as older counterparts. ... If the Eighth Amendment set forth an ordinary rule of law, it would indeed be the role of this Court to say what the law is. But the Court having pronounced that the Eighth Amendment is an ever-changing reflection of "the evolving standards of decency" of our society, it makes no sense for the Justices then to prescribe those standards rather than discern them from the practices of our people. On the evolving-standards hypothesis, the only legitimate function of this Court is to identify a moral consensus of the American people. By what conceivable warrant can nine lawyers presume to be the authoritative conscience of the Nation? (*Roper v. Simmons*, 112 S. W. 3d 397, affirmed, [2005])

Well, you know maybe 60 years or so ago we adopted, first in the Eighth Amendment area cruel and unusual punishment the notion that the Constitution is not static. It doesn't mean what the people voted for when it was ratified. It doesn't mean that. Rather, it changes from era to era to comport with — and this is a quote from our cases, "the evolving standards of decency that mark the progress of a maturing society." I detest that phrase ... because I'm afraid that societies don't always mature. Sometimes they rot. What makes you think that, you know, human progress is one upwardly inclined plane, every day and every way we get better and better? It seems to me that the purpose of the Bill of Rights was to prevent change, not to encourage it and have it written into a Constitution. (Remarks at U.S. Association of Constitutional Law Discussion, Washington, DC, 1/13/05)

Today's opinion provides a perfect example of why judges are ill equipped to make the type of legislative judgments the Court insists on making here. To support its opinion that States should be prohibited from imposing the death penalty on anyone who committed murder before age 18, the Court looks to scientific and sociological studies, picking and choosing those that support its position. It never explains why those particular studies are methodologically sound; none was ever entered into evidence or tested in an adversarial proceeding. (*Roper v. Simmons*, 112 S. W. 3d 397, affirmed, [(2005)])

Not the Court's call

Constitutional Interpretation. It is however an important one. I was vividly reminded how important it was last week when the Court came out with a controversial decision in the *Roper* case. And I watched one television commentary on the case in which the host had one person defending the opinion on the ground that people should not be subjected to capital punishment for crimes they commit when they are younger than eighteen, and the other person attacked the opinion on the ground that a jury should be able to decide that a person, despite the fact he was under eighteen, given the crime, given the person involved, should be subjected to capital punishment. And it struck me how irrelevant it was, how much the point had been missed. The question wasn't whether the call was right or wrong. The important question was who should make the call. (Remarks at the Woodrow Wilson Center, Washington, DC, 3/14/05*)*

Constitution becomes Justices' "current personal views"

In a system based upon constitutional and statutory text democratically adopted, the concept of "law" ordinarily signifies that particular words have a fixed meaning. Such law does not change, and this Court's pronouncement of it therefore remains authoritative until (confessing our prior error) we overrule. The Court has purported to make of the Eighth Amendment, however, a mirror of the passing and changing sentiment of American society regarding penology. ... We must disregard the new reality that, to the extent our Eighth Amendment decisions constitute something more than a show of hands on the current Justices' current personal views about penology, they purport to be nothing more than a snapshot of American public opinion at a particular point in time (with the time-frames now shortened to a mere 15 years). We must treat these decisions just as though they represented real law, real prescriptions democratically adopted by the American people, as conclusively (rather than sequentially) construed by this Court. ... The result will be to crown arbitrariness with chaos. (*Roper v. Simmons*, 112 S. W. 3d 397, affirmed, [2005])

Today's decision is the pinnacle of our Eighth Amendment death-is-different jurisprudence. Not only does it, like all of that jurisprudence, find no support in the text or history of the Eighth Amendment; it does not even have support in current social attitudes regarding the conditions that render an otherwise just death penalty inappropriate. Seldom has an opinion of this Court rested so obviously upon nothing but the personal views of its members. (*Atkins v. Virginia*, 536 U.S. 304 [2002])

Moral obligation on voters and legislators

Capital cases are much different from the other life-and-death issues that my Court sometimes faces: abortion, for example, or legalized suicide. There it is not the state of which I am, in a sense, the last instrument that is decreeing death, but rather private individuals whom the state has decided not to restrain. One may argue, as many do, that the society has a moral obligation to restrain them. That moral obligation may weigh heavily upon the voter and upon the legislator who enacts the laws, but a judge, I think, bears no moral guilt for the laws society has failed to enact. (Remarks at Pew Forum Conference, Chicago, IL, 1/25/02)

Death penalty undone by proponents of "living Constitution"

I pause at this point to call attention to the fact that, in my view, the choice for the judge who believes the death penalty to be immoral is resignation rather than simply ignoring duly enacted constitutional laws and sabotaging the death penalty. He has, after all, taken an oath to apply those laws, and has been given no power to supplant them with rules of his own. Of course, if he feels strongly enough, he can go beyond mere resignation and lead a political campaign to abolish the death penalty, and if that fails, lead a revolution. But rewrite the laws he cannot do. This dilemma, of course, need not be faced by proponents of the living Constitution who believe that it means what it ought to mean. If the death penalty is immoral, then it is surely unconstitutional, and one can continue to sit while nullifying the death penalty. You can see why the living Constitution has such attraction for us judges. (Remarks at Pew Forum Conference, Chicago, IL, 1/25/02)

Court pays lipservice to legislative "national consensus"

The Court is left to argue, therefore, that execution of the mildly retarded is inconsistent with the "evolving standards of decency that mark the progress of a maturing society." Before today, our opinions consistently emphasized that Eighth Amendment judgments regarding the existence of social "standards" "should be informed by objective factors to the maximum possible extent" and "should not be, or appear to be, merely the subjective views of individual Justices." "First" among these objective factors are the "statutes passed by society's elected representatives," because it "will rarely if ever be the case that the Members of this Court will have a better sense of the evolution in views of the American people than do their elected representatives." The Court pays lipservice to these precedents as it miraculously extracts a "national consensus" forbidding execution of the mentally retarded. … (*Atkins v. Virginia*, 536 U.S. 304 [2002])

Court ignores juries

The fact that juries continue to sentence mentally retarded offenders to death for extreme crimes shows that society's moral outrage sometimes demands execution of retarded offenders. By what principle of law, science, or logic can the Court pronounce that this is wrong? (*Atkins v. Virginia*, 536 U.S. 304 [2002])

Sixteen years ago, this Court decreed — by a sheer act of will, with no pretense of foundation in constitutional text or American tradition — that the People (as in We, the People) cannot decree the death penalty, absolutely and categorically, for any criminal act, even (presumably) genocide; the jury must always be given the option of extending mercy. Today, obscured within the fog of confusion that is our annually improvised Eighth-Amendment, "death-is-different" jurisprudence, the Court strikes a further blow against the People in its campaign against the death penalty. Not only must mercy be allowed, but now only the merciful may be permitted to sit in judgment. Those who agree with the author of Exodus, or with Immanuel Kant, must be banished from American juries — not because the People have so decreed, but because such jurors do not share the strong penological preferences of this Court. In my view, that not only is not required by the Constitution of the United States; it grossly offends it. (*Morgan v. Illinois*, 504 U.S. 719 [1992])

Mitigating evidence requirement a "mockery"

In my view this Court has no colorable basis, either in constitutional text or in national tradition, for imposing upon the States a further constitutional requirement that the sentencer consider mitigating evidence. As this and other cases upon our docket amply show, that recently invented requirement has introduced not only a mandated arbitrariness quite inconsistent with Furman, but also an impenetrable complexity and hence a propensity to error that make a scandal and a mockery of the capital sentencing process. (*Richmond v. Lewis*, 506 U.S. 56 [1992])

CHAPTER 13

Constitutional Crime and Punishment

*Judicial conservatives are charged with
upholding the constitutional rights of the accused and
convicted as well as the constitutional powers
of the criminal justice system.*

The Living Constitution, like the legislatures that enacted these laws, would have allowed sentencing factors to be determined by the judge because all the Living Constitution assures you is that what will happen is what a majority wants to happen. And that's not the purpose of constitutional guarantees.

Justice Antonin Scalia, March 14, 2005

"These regulations [prohibiting disruptive and violent prisoners access to newspapers and magazines]are reasonably related to the legitimate penological goal of curbing prison misconduct, and I would therefore affirm the decision of the District Court."

Samuel Alito, *Dissent, Banks v. Beard,* 2005.

*I*n the 1960s while Earl Warren was chief justice, the Supreme Court began to expand the rights of criminals, especially in the area of evidentiary and police matters. The complicated Miranda rule was manufactured by the Court, and more criminals began finding loopholes to escape punishment. At times, these policies have crippled the police and criminal justice systems.

While respecting the right of the accused to a speedy and fair trial, Justice Antonin Scalia has ruled in favor of strictly interpreting the Constitution when it comes to criminal law. In an era of mounting crime, it is vital for any judge or justice to ensure that a proper balance exists between the constitutional rights of individuals and the necessary constitutional powers of the police and criminal systems to enforce the law. This is the ideal for judicial conservatives. Let's explore the Scalia model on this issue. —S.E.

<u>The Scalia Model on Constitutional Crime and Punishment</u>

Right to trial by jury

In a series of cases, the Court had seemingly acknowledged that you didn't have to have trial by jury of the facts that increase your sentence. You can make the increased sentence a "sentencing factor" — you get 30 years for burglary, but if the burglary is committed with a gun, as a sentencing factor the judge can give you another 10 years. And the judge will decide whether you used a gun. And he will decide it, not beyond a reasonable doubt, but whether it's more likely than not. Well, we held recently, I'm happy to say, that this violates the right to a trial by jury. The Living Constitution would not have produced that result. The Living Constitution, like the legislatures that enacted these laws, would have allowed sentencing factors to be determined by the judge because all the Living Constitution assures you is that what will happen is what the majority wants to happen. And that's not the purpose of constitutional guarantees." (Remarks at the Woodrow Wilson Center, Washington, DC, 3/14/05)

When I find that the original meaning of the jury trial guarantee is that any additional time you spend in prison which depends upon a fact must depend upon a fact found by a jury — once I find that's what the jury trial guarantee means, I am handcuffed. (Remarks at the Woodrow Wilson Center, Washington, DC, 3/14/05)

Stretching the Fourth Amendment "beyond its words"

In California v. Hodari, *a suspect who dropped a rock of cocaine during a police pursuit sought to have the cocaine disqualified as evidence on the grounds it was obtained during an unlawful seizure. Scalia writes:*

The language of the Fourth Amendment, of course, cannot sustain respondent's contention. The word "seizure" readily bears the meaning of a laying on of hands or application of physical force to restrain movement, even when it is ultimately unsuccessful. … It does not remotely apply, however, to the prospect of a policeman yelling "Stop, in the name of the law!" at a fleeing form that continues to flee. That is no seizure. … An arrest requires either physical force … or, where that is absent, submission to the assertion of authority. … We do not think it desirable, even as a policy matter, to stretch the Fourth

Amendment beyond its words and beyond the meaning of arrest, as respondent urges. (*California v. Hodari*, 499 U.S. 621 [1991])

Constitution requires "reasonable judgment" from law enforcement

In Illinois v. Rodriguez, *a suspect had been arrested for "possession of illegal drugs, which the police had observed in plain view and seized. The officers did not have an arrest or search warrant, but gained entry to the apartment with the assistance of" a woman who claimed she lived there. She opened the door with a key and gave the officers permission to enter the apartment. The Court ruled that although the woman did not in reality live in the apartment, there was no illegal entry by the police because they "reasonably believed at the time of their entry that she possessed the authority to consent." Scalia writes:*

The Fourth Amendment generally prohibits the warrantless entry of a person's home, whether to make an arrest or to search for specific objects. The prohibition does not apply, however, to situations in which voluntary consent has been obtained, either from the individual whose property is searched, or from a third party who possesses common authority over the premises. ... Whether the basis for such authority [to enter a home] exists is the sort of recurring factual question to which law enforcement officials must be expected to apply their judgment, and all the Fourth Amendment requires is that they answer it reasonably. The Constitution is no[t] violated when officers enter without a warrant because they reasonably (though erroneously) believe that the person who has consented to their entry.... (*Illinois v. Rodriguez*, 497 U.S. 177 [1990])

On the right to confront your accusers

Recently, last term, we reversed a 15-year-old decision of the Court, which had held that the Confrontation Clause — which couldn't be clearer, it says, "In all criminal prosecutions, the accused shall enjoy the right ... to be confronted with the witness against him." But a Living Constitution Court held that all that was necessary to comply with the Confrontation Clause was that the hearsay evidence which is introduced — hearsay evidence means you can't cross-examine the person who said it because he's not in the court — the hearsay evidence has to bear indicia of reliability. I'm happy to say that we reversed it last term with the votes of the two originalists on the Court. And the opinion said that the only indicium of reliability that the Confrontation Clause acknowledges is confrontation. You bring the witness in to testify and to be cross-examined. (Remarks at the Woodrow Wilson Center, Washington, DC, 3/14/05)

Regarding police interrogation

In Minnick v. Mississippi, *the Court ruled to disqualify a murder confession on the grounds the suspect was not properly informed of his rights. The initial interrogation of the suspect ended when he requested counsel. But after the suspect communicated with a lawyer, the police restarted the interrogation, telling the suspect he could not refuse to talk to them. The Court ruled that counsel must be "present" not simply "consulted." Scalia dissented, writing:*

The Court today establishes an irrebuttable presumption that a criminal suspect, after invoking his Miranda right to counsel, can never validly waive that right during any police-initiated encounter, even after the suspect has been provided multiple Miranda warnings and has actually consulted his attorney. ... [The classification of an involuntary confession] should not, in my view, extend beyond the circumstances ... where the suspect in custody asked to consult an attorney, and was interrogated before that attorney had ever been provided. ... After a suspect has seen his request for an attorney honored, however, and has actually spoken with that attorney, the probabilities change. The suspect then knows that he has an advocate on his side, and that the police will permit him to consult that advocate. He almost certainly also has a heightened awareness (above what the Miranda warning itself will provide) of his right to remain silent...." (*Minnick v. Mississippi*, 498 U.S. 146 [1990])

CHAPTER 14

Reconnecting "General" to Welfare

A judicial conservative understands that the Constitution's "general welfare" provision places limitations on the modern welfare state.

The issue is not whether there should be provision for the poor but rather the degree to which that provision should be made through coercive power of the State. Christ said, after all, that you should give your goods to the poor. Not that you should force someone else to give his.

Justice Antonin Scalia, May 2, 1996

"I believe very strongly in…limited government, federalism… the supremacy of the elected branches of government."

Samuel Alito, 1985

The preamble of the Constitution establishes promoting the "general welfare" as one of the foundational purposes of the creation of the document. But what does this phrase, "promote the general welfare," mean, and does the modern welfare state resemble that original meaning?

Since President Franklin Roosevelt implemented his New Deal during the Great Depression, "general welfare" has taken on a new and expansive meaning. As a result, the United States has essentially operated a capitalist economy within a socialist public entitlement framework. Thus, the welfare state has flourished, along with programs like Medicaid, Medicare, and Social Security. But does the Constitution allow for or endorse the welfare state within the concept of "general welfare"? Antonin Scalia thinks not and he has set out a challenging model for judicial conservatives to follow in this century. How Samuel Alito rules in such cases could determine the economic destiny of our nation. —S.E.

The Scalia Model on Reconnecting "General" to Welfare

"We are all socialists"

[I]n a modern context … we are all socialists. In the United States that battle was fought and decided in the 1930s with the so-called New

Deal of Franklin Roosevelt. No one, even in the most conservative quarters of American society, any longer opposes the welfare state, which provides many benefits and social services to individual citizens. The only real argument is over how numerous those benefits and social services ought to be and how poor one should be in order to qualify. ... (Remarks at Pontifical Gregorian University, Rome, Italy, 5/2/96)

Redefining the "general welfare"

We now believe that any expenditure for any citizen is an expenditure for the general welfare: whether to the poor, such as the recipients of food stamps, which is what the American welfare system provides; or to the middle class or even fairly well-to-do, such as federal assistance to the victims of a tornado in a very elegant section of Florida; or even assistance to the downright rich, such as the shareholders of the Chrysler Corporation, whom we bailed out. All of these are now regarded as entirely proper objects of the state's beneficence. (Remarks at Pontifical Gregorian University, Rome, Italy, 5/2/96)

Welfare and coercive power

Now, the allure of socialism ... is that it means well. It is, or appears to be at least, altruistic. It promises assistance from the state for the poor and public provision for all the necessities of life: from maternity care to geriatric care, and from kindergarten through university. Capitalism, on the other hand, laissez-faire capitalism, promises nothing from the state, except security of person and property, and the opportunity to succeed or fail. Adam Smith points unabashedly to the fact that the baker does not provide bread out of the goodness of his heart but for profit. How uninspiring.

Yet if you reflect upon it you will see that the socialistic message is not necessarily Christian, and the capitalistic message is not necessarily non-Christian. The issue is not whether there should be provision for the poor but rather the degree to which that provision should be made

through the coercive power of the state. Christ said, after all, that you should give your goods to the poor. Not that you should force someone else to give his. One should not forget that the individual voter in a socialist democracy votes not to give his own goods to the needy but also to force others to do so. They will go to jail for tax evasion if they refuse. And often, as I shall observe later, the needy is him: the voter. ...
(Remarks at Pontifical Gregorian University, Rome, Italy, 5/2/96)

Welfare and Christianity

The question I am asking is whether Christian faith must incline us toward that system, and the answer ... is no. Christ did not preach a chicken in every pot or the elimination of poverty in our lifetime. ... His message, the Christian message as I understand it, is not the need to eliminate hunger or misery or misfortune, but rather, the need for each individual to love and help the hungry, the miserable, the unfortunate.

Indeed, the argument can be made that far from doing Christ's work, state provision of welfare positively impedes it. To the extent the state takes upon itself one of the corporal works of mercy that could and would have been undertaken privately, it deprives individuals of an opportunity ... for the interchange of love among its members. ... What need for me to give a beggar a handout? Do I not pay taxes for government food stamps and municipally run shelters and soup kitchens? ...
(Remarks at Pontifical Gregorian University, Rome, Italy, 5/2/96)

"Governmentalization of charity"

There is, of course, neither any love nor any merit in the taxes I pay for those services. I pay them under compulsion. And it can be argued the governmentalization of charity affects not just the donor, but also the recipient. What was once asked as a favor is now demanded as an entitlement. ...

This belief must affect the character of welfare recipients.... It is humbling to be an object of charity.... The transformation of charity into legal entitlement has produced both donors without love and recipients without gratitude. It has also produced a change in the product that is distributed. ...

The religiously driven and religiously funded social welfare movements of the 19th century sought to achieve not merely the alleviation of poverty and hardship, but also what was called moral uplift. Of course that is no part of state-administrated social welfare today. ... And the result is often the elimination of poverty without the elimination of the vices that produce the poverty — indeed, sometimes with a positive reinforcement of those vices, through elimination of the pain that they ordinarily produce.... (Remarks at Pontifical Gregorian University, Rome, Italy, 5/2/96)

Welfare actually "goes to the middle class"

Finally, I may mention that even the seemingly Christian virtue of socialism, namely that it means well and seeks to help the poor, may be greatly exaggerated. It is true in the United States, and I believe it is true in all of the Western democracies, that the vast bulk of social spending does not go to the poor, but rather to the middle class, which also happens to be the class most numerous at the polls. The most expensive entitlement programs in the United States, Social Security and Medicare, which is public medical assistance, for example, overwhelmingly benefit those who are not in dire financial straits. So one may plausibly argue that welfare-state democracy does not even really have the Christian virtue of altruism. The majority does not say to the rich, "Give your money to the poor" but rather, "Give your money to us". ... (Remarks at Pontifical Gregorian University, Rome, Italy, 5/2/96)

CHAPTER 15

Color-Blind Constitution

Upholding a color-blind Constitution, in spite of the most "affirmative" actions and intentions, is the judicial conservative's goal.

In my view, government can never have a "compelling interest" in
discriminating on the basis of race in order to "make up" for past racial
discrimination in the opposite direction. Individuals who have been wronged
by unlawful racial discrimination should be made whole; but under our
Constitution there can be no such thing as either a creditor or a debtor race.
That concept is alien to the Constitution's focus upon the individual.
Justice Antonin Scalia, *Adarand Constructors v. Pena,* 1995

"I am particularly proud of my contributions in recent cases in
which the government has argued in the Supreme Court that
racial and ethnic quotas should not be allowed."
Samuel Alito, 1985

Affirmative action was first introduced as a policy by President Lyndon Johnson in 1965 as a remedy for racial inequality. In particular focusing on education for jobs, affirmative action involves taking active measures to increase the representation of minorities in employment and education placements. The problem of "reverse discrimination" soon became an issue. While government affirmative action policies were attempting to create ethnic equity in employment, non-minority students and applicants began to be denied jobs, scholarships, or admission to educational institutes in favor of minority candidates. The tables were turned.

Justice Scalia argues that there is never any justification for discrimination by race even to make up for the effects of past discrimination. He acknowledges racial discrimination is a problem, but points out the solution cannot be one which still classifies according to race. The Constitution is and should be color-blind. This is the high standard judicial conservatives and all judges and justices must uphold. Fortunately for Samuel Alito and others, the Scalia model proves to be an excellent guardian of the color-blind Constitution. —S.E.

The Scalia Model on Color-Blind Constitution

"Just one race...American"

In my view, government can never have a "compelling interest" in discriminating on the basis of race in order to "make up" for past racial discrimination in the opposite direction. Individuals who have been wronged by unlawful racial discrimination should be made whole; but under our Constitution there can be no such thing as either a creditor or a debtor race. That concept is alien to the Constitution's focus upon the individual. To pursue the concept of racial entitlement — even for the most admirable and benign of purposes — is to reinforce and preserve for future mischief the way of thinking that produced race slavery, race privilege and race hatred. In the eyes of government, we are just one race here. It is American. (*Adarand Constructors v. Pena*, 515 U.S. 200 [1995])

Any race classifications "fatal to a Nation"

I do not agree ... that, despite the Fourteenth Amendment, state and local governments may in some circumstances discriminate on the basis of race in order (in a broad sense) "to ameliorate the effects of past discrimination." The benign purpose of compensating for social disadvantages, whether they have been acquired by reason of prior discrimination or otherwise, can no more be pursued by the illegitimate means of racial discrimination than can other assertedly benign purposes we have repeatedly rejected. The difficulty of overcoming the effects of past discrimination is as nothing compared with the difficulty of eradicating from our society the source of those effects, which is the tendency - fatal to a Nation such as ours - to classify and judge men and women on the basis of their country of origin or the color of their skin. A solution to the first problem that aggravates the second is no solution at all. (*Richmond v. J. A. Croson Co.*, 488 U. S. 469, 520 [1989])

Permissible ways to "undo the effects of past discrimination"

A State can, of course, act "to undo the effects of past discrimination" in many permissible ways that do not involve classification by race. In the particular field of state contracting, for example, it may adopt a preference for small businesses, or even for new businesses - which would make it easier for those previously excluded by discrimination to enter the field. Such programs may well have racially disproportionate impact, but they are not based on race. And, of course, a State may "undo the effects of past discrimination" in the sense of giving the identified victim of state discrimination that which it wrongfully denied him — for example, giving to a previously rejected black applicant the job that, by reason of discrimination, had been awarded to a white applicant, even if this means terminating the latter's employment. In such a context, the white jobholder is not being selected for disadvantageous treatment because of his race, but because he was wrongfully awarded a job to which another is entitled. That is worlds apart from the system here, in which those to be disadvantaged are identified solely by race. (*Richmond v. J. A. Croson Co.*, 488 U. S. 469, 520 [1989])

Excusing the "sham" of racially proportionate admissions

I join the opinion of The Chief Justice. As he demonstrates, the University of Michigan Law School's mystical "critical mass" justification for its discrimination by race challenges even the most gullible mind. The admissions statistics show it to be a sham to cover a scheme of racially proportionate admissions. ... I add the following: The "educational benefit" that the University of Michigan seeks to achieve by racial discrimination consists, according to the Court, of "cross-racial understanding," "better prepar[ation of] students for an increasingly diverse workforce and society," all of which is necessary not only for work, but also for good "citizenship." This is not, of course, an "educational benefit" on which students will be graded on their Law

School transcript (Works and Plays Well with Others: B+) or tested by the bar examiners (Q: Describe in 500 words or less your cross-racial understanding). For it is a lesson of life rather than law — essentially the same lesson taught to (or rather learned by, for it cannot be "taught" in the usual sense) people three feet shorter and twenty years younger than the full-grown adults at the University of Michigan Law School, in institutions ranging from Boy Scout troops to public-school kindergartens. If properly considered an "educational benefit" at all, it is surely not one that is either uniquely relevant to law school or uniquely "teachable" in a formal educational setting. And therefore: If it is appropriate for the University of Michigan Law School to use racial discrimination for the purpose of putting together a "critical mass" that will convey generic lessons in socialization and good citizenship, surely it is no less appropriate — indeed, particularly appropriate — for the civil service system of the State of Michigan to do so. There, also, those exposed to "critical masses" of certain races will presumably become better Americans, better Michiganders, better civil servants. And surely private employers cannot be criticized — indeed, should be praised — if they also "teach" good citizenship to their adult employees through a patriotic, all-American system of racial discrimination in hiring. The nonminority individuals who are deprived of a legal education, a civil service job, or any job at all by reason of their skin color will surely understand. (*Grutter v. Bollinger*, 288 F.3d 732, affirmed [2003])

CHAPTER 16

Extracting the Courts from the Culture War

Where the Constitution is silent, federal judges and justices should work to return questions of culture and morality to the people.

The Court has taken sides in the culture war, departing from its role of assuring, as neutral observer, that the democratic rules of engagement are observed.
Justice Antonin Scalia, *Romer v. Evans*, 1996

"The Supreme Court's past and future difficulties are the wages of insisting that the Constitution answer a question that should be entrusted to the mundane processes of democratic government."
Samuel Alito, 1988

A merica is in the grips of a great cultural struggle, often called a "culture war." To those living at the dawn of this new millennium, it seems the struggle is more intense and more animated than in prior times. A brief read of American history reveals that great cultural conflicts have always been playing out in our society. The difference is that today, federal judges —not the people, their representatives, or the Constitution —have the final say on seemingly all cultural questions. As Antonin Scalia has noted, the Court "has taken sides in the culture war."

While Scalia may have strong personal opinions on questions of culture, as a Supreme Court justice he has consistently worked to uphold the Constitution on such questions, and where the Constitution is silent, allow the people and their representatives to make moral choices and distinctions as they deem fit. Law is based on morality, and as Scalia notes the people have the right to frown on sodomy the same way they disapprove of prostitution or incest. They also have a right to amend the Constitution to create a "right" to sodomy or incest or prostitution. The Scalia model is an excellent guide for every judicial conservative and will help restore order to our current cultural conflict. It's time to take the courts out of the culture war and return these struggles, where the Constitution is silent, to the people. —S.E.

The Scalia Model on Extracting the Courts from the Culture War

"Court has taken sides in the culture wars"

One of the most revealing statements in today's opinion is the Court's grim warning that the criminalization of homosexual conduct is "an invitation to subject homosexual persons to discrimination both in the public and in the private spheres." It is clear from this that the Court has taken sides in the culture war, departing from its role of assuring, as neutral observer, that the democratic rules of engagement are observed. (*Lawrence v. Texas*, 41 S. W. 3d 349, reversed and remanded [2003])

When the Court takes sides in the culture wars, it tends to be with the knights rather than the villains — and more specifically with the Templars, reflecting the views and values of the lawyer class from which the Court's Members are drawn. How that class feels about homosexuality will be evident to anyone who wishes to interview job applicants at virtually any of the Nation's law schools. The interviewer may refuse to offer a job because the applicant is a Republican; because he is an adulterer; because he went to the wrong prep school or belongs to the wrong country club; because he eats snails; because he is a womanizer; because she wears real-animal fur; or even because he hates the Chicago Cubs. But if the interviewer should wish not to be an associate or partner of an applicant because he disapproves of the applicant's homosexuality, then he will have violated the pledge which the Association of American Law Schools requires all its member-schools to exact from job interviewers: "assurance of the employer's willingness" to hire homosexuals. (*Romer v. Evans*, 517 U.S. 620 [1996])

Court's actions not judicial judgment, but "political will"

Today's opinion has no foundation in American constitutional law, and barely pretends to. The people of Colorado have adopted an entirely reasonable provision which does not even disfavor homosexuals in any substantive sense, but merely denies them preferential treatment.

Amendment 2 is designed to prevent piecemeal deterioration of the sexual morality favored by a majority of Coloradans, and is not only an appropriate means to that legitimate end, but a means that Americans have employed before. Striking it down is an act, not of judicial judgment, but of political will. (*Romer v. Evans*, 517 U.S. 620 [1996])

People, not courts, should debate and decide cultural questions

Let me be clear that I have nothing against homosexuals, or any other group, promoting their agenda through normal democratic means. Social perceptions of sexual and other morality change over time, and every group has the right to persuade its fellow citizens that its view of such matters is the best. That homosexuals have achieved some success in that enterprise is attested to by the fact that Texas is one of the few remaining States that criminalize private, consensual homosexual acts. But persuading one's fellow citizens is one thing, and imposing one's views in absence of democratic majority will is something else. I would no more require a State to criminalize homosexual acts — or, for that matter, display any moral disapprobation of them — than I would forbid it to do so. What Texas has chosen to do is well within the range of traditional democratic action, and its hand should not be stayed through the invention of a brand-new "constitutional right" by a Court that is impatient of democratic change. It is indeed true that "later generations can see that laws once thought necessary and proper in fact serve only to oppress," and when that happens, later generations can repeal those laws. But it is the premise of our system that those judgments are to be made by the people, and not imposed by a governing caste that knows best. (*Lawrence v. Texas*, 41 S. W. 3d 349, reversed and remanded [2003])

Laws can be based on moral choices

State laws against bigamy, same-sex marriage, adult incest, prostitution, masturbation, adultery, fornication, bestiality, and obscenity are likewise sustainable only in light of *Bowers'* validation of laws based on moral choices. Every single one of these laws is called into question by today's decision; the Court makes no effort to cabin the scope of its decision to exclude them from its holding. ... "The law," it said, "is constantly based on notions of morality, and if all laws representing essentially moral choices are to be invalidated under the Due Process Clause, the courts will be very busy indeed." (*Lawrence v. Texas*, 41 S. W. 3d 349, reversed and remanded [2003])

Most of the rest of today's opinion has no relevance to its actual holding — that the Texas statute "furthers no legitimate state interest which can justify" its application to petitioners under rational-basis review. Though there is discussion of "fundamental proposition[s]," and "fundamental decisions," nowhere does the Court's opinion declare that homosexual sodomy is a "fundamental right" under the Due Process Clause; nor does it subject the Texas law to the standard of review that would be appropriate (strict scrutiny) if homosexual sodomy were a "fundamental right." (*Lawrence v. Texas*, 41 S. W. 3d 349, reversed and remanded [2003])

States can prosecute "in matters pertaining to sex"

States continue to prosecute all sorts of crimes by adults "in matters pertaining to sex": prostitution, adult incest, adultery, obscenity, and child pornography. Sodomy laws, too, have been enforced "in the past half century," in which there have been 134 reported cases involving prosecutions for consensual, adult, homosexual sodomy. ... Constitutional entitlements do not spring into existence because some States choose to lessen or eliminate criminal sanctions on certain behavior. Much less do they spring into existence, as the Court seems to believe, because foreign nations decriminalize conduct. (*Lawrence v. Texas*, 41 S. W. 3d 349, reversed and remanded [2003])

Citizens can make moral choices and discriminations

Many Americans do not want persons who openly engage in homosexual conduct as partners in their business, as scoutmasters for their children, as teachers in their children's schools, or as boarders in their home. They view this as protecting themselves and their families from a lifestyle that they believe to be immoral and destructive. The Court views it as "discrimination" which it is the function of our judgments to deter. So imbued is the Court with the law profession's anti-anti-homosexual culture, that it is seemingly unaware that the attitudes of that culture are not obviously "mainstream"; that in most States what the Court calls "discrimination" against those who engage in homosexual acts is perfectly legal; that proposals to ban such "discrimination" under Title VII have repeatedly been rejected by Congress; that in some cases such "discrimination" is mandated by federal statute; and that in some cases such "discrimination" is a constitutional right. ... (*Lawrence v. Texas*, 41 S. W. 3d 349, reversed and remanded [2003])

The Court's opinion contains grim, disapproving hints that Coloradans have been guilty of "animus" or "animosity" toward homosexuality, as though that has been established as Unamerican. Of course it is our moral heritage that one should not hate any human being or class of human beings. But I had thought that one could consider certain conduct reprehensible — murder, for example, or polygamy, or cruelty to animals — and could exhibit even "animus" toward such conduct. Surely that is the only sort of "animus" at issue here: moral disapproval of homosexual conduct, the same sort of moral disapproval that produced the centuries-old criminal laws that we held constitutional in *Bowers*. (*Romer v. Evans*, 517 U.S. 620 [1996])

The Court's portrayal of Coloradans as a society fallen victim to pointless, hate-filled "gay-bashing" is so false as to be comical. Colorado not only is one of the 25 States that have repealed their anti-sodomy laws, but was among the first to do so. But the society that eliminates criminal punishment for homosexual acts does not necessarily abandon the view that homosexuality is morally wrong and socially harmful; often, abolition simply reflects the view that enforcement of such criminal laws involves unseemly intrusion into the intimate lives of citizens. (*Romer v. Evans*, 517 U.S. 620 [1996])

Court marks "the end of all morals legislation"

The Texas statute undeniably seeks to further the belief of its citizens that certain forms of sexual behavior are "immoral and unacceptable," the same interest furthered by criminal laws against fornication, bigamy, adultery, adult incest, bestiality, and obscenity. *Bowers* held that this was a legitimate state interest. The Court today reaches the opposite conclusion. The Texas statute, it says, "furthers no legitimate state interest which can justify its intrusion into the personal and private life of the individual." The Court embraces instead Justice Stevens' declaration in his *Bowers* dissent, that "the fact that the governing majority in a State has traditionally viewed a particular practice as immoral is not a sufficient reason for upholding a law prohibiting the practice." This effectively decrees the end of all morals legislation. If, as the Court asserts, the promotion of majoritarian sexual morality is not even a legitimate state interest, none of the above-mentioned laws can survive rational-basis review. (*Lawrence v. Texas*, 41 S. W. 3d 349, reversed and remanded [2003])

CHAPTER 17

Marriage and the Homosexual Agenda

Judicial conservatives must resist the Court's promotion of the homosexual agenda and support the people's right to decide this crucial issue.

Today's opinion is the product of a Court, which is the product of a law-profession culture, that has largely signed on to the so-called homosexual agenda, by which I mean the agenda promoted by some homosexual activists directed at eliminating the moral opprobrium that has traditionally attached to homosexual conduct.
Justice Antonin Scalia, *Lawrence v. Texas*, 2003

"The Policy, then, appears to cover substantially more speech than could be prohibited under Tinker's substantial disruption test."
Samuel Alito, *Saxe v. State College*, 2000 (a case in which a school policy prohibited students from discussing their religious beliefs pertaining to homosexuality was overturned)

F or thousands of years, marriage has been defined as the union of one man and one woman. For both moral and practical considerations, the state has preferred marriage in law and policy. This legal preference is clearly justified. The importance of a child receiving the care of a mother and a father has consistently been proven by studies. Today, the future of marriage is the central debate of the cultural conflict discussed previously in this book. Will one-man, one-woman marriage continue to be preferred, or will it be essentially destroyed by the creation of a "right" to homosexuality and same-sex marriage?

Over recent decades the Supreme Court established a platform for this debate by creating and then expanding a "right of privacy" pertaining to sexual activities. The homosexual movement has used this open door to chip away, through the courts, at the distinctions between hetero- and homo-sexual relations. It is now clear where the courts are heading – we have arrived at the brink of a full-blown constitutional right to homosexuality and same-sex marriage created by fiat through judicial action. Meanwhile, the people and their legislatures continue to affirm their right to draw such distinctions and safeguard marriage in our culture. The showdown is upon us, and the courts want the final say. Antonin Scalia finds no constitutional right to homosexual relations in the Constitution. He also believes the people, not unelected judges, have the power to decide the definition and meaning of marriage. The Scalia model is the standard for judicial conservatives, including Samuel Alito. —S.E.

The Scalia Model on Marriage and the Homosexual Agenda

Homosexuality "not a right 'deeply rooted in our Nation's history and tradition'"

Whether homosexual sodomy was prohibited by a law targeted at same-sex sexual relations or by a more general law prohibiting both homosexual and heterosexual sodomy, the only relevant point is that it was criminalized — which suffices to establish that homosexual sodomy is not a right "deeply rooted in our Nation's history and tradition." (*Lawrence v. Texas*, 41 S. W. 3d 349, reversed and remanded [2003])

Constitution "says nothing about this subject"

In holding that homosexuality cannot be singled out for disfavorable treatment, the Court contradicts a decision, unchallenged here, pronounced only 10 years ago, and places the prestige of this institution behind the proposition that opposition to homosexuality is as reprehensible as racial or religious bias. Whether it is or not is precisely the cultural debate that gave rise to the Colorado constitutional amendment (and to the preferential laws against which the amendment was directed). Since the Constitution of the United States says nothing about this subject, it is left to be resolved by normal democratic means, including the democratic adoption of provisions in state constitutions. (*Romer v. Evans*, 517 U.S. 620 (1996))

Court has "no business imposing"

This Court has no business imposing upon all Americans the resolution favored by the elite class from which the Members of this institution are selected, pronouncing that "animosity" toward homosexuality is evil." (*Romer v. Evans*, 517 U.S. 620 [1996])

Court has "signed on to the so-called homosexual agenda"

Today's opinion is the product of a Court, which is the product of a law-profession culture, that has largely signed on to the so-called homosexual agenda, by which I mean the agenda promoted by some homosexual activists directed at eliminating the moral opprobrium that has traditionally attached to homosexual conduct. I noted in an earlier opinion the fact that the American Association of Law Schools (to which any reputable law school must seek to belong) excludes from membership any school that refuses to ban from its job-interview facilities a law firm (no matter how small) that does not wish to hire as a prospective partner a person who openly engages in homosexual conduct. (*Lawrence v. Texas*, 41 S. W. 3d 349, reversed and remanded [2003])

Court is creating a constitutional right to homosexuality

The people may feel that their disapprobation of homosexual conduct is strong enough to disallow homosexual marriage, but not strong enough to criminalize private homosexual acts — and may legislate accordingly. The Court today pretends that it possesses a similar freedom of action, so that we need not fear judicial imposition of homosexual marriage, as has recently occurred in Canada. ... At the end of its opinion — after having laid waste the foundations of our rational-basis jurisprudence — the Court says that the present case "does not involve whether the government must give formal recognition to any relationship that homosexual persons seek to enter." Do not believe it. More illuminating than this bald, unreasoned disclaimer is the progression of thought displayed by an earlier passage in the Court's opinion, which notes the constitutional protections afforded to "personal decisions relating to marriage, procreation, contraception, family relationships, child rearing, and education," and then declares that "[p]ersons in a homosexual relationship may seek autonomy for these purposes, just as heterosexual persons do." (*Lawrence v. Texas*, 41 S. W. 3d 349, reversed and remanded [2003])

Court dismantles distinction between hetero- and homo-sexual

Today's opinion dismantles the structure of constitutional law that has permitted a distinction to be made between heterosexual and homosexual unions, insofar as formal recognition in marriage is concerned. If moral disapprobation of homosexual conduct is "no legitimate state interest" for purposes of proscribing that conduct; and if, as the Court coos (casting aside all pretense of neutrality), "[w]hen sexuality finds overt expression in intimate conduct with another person, the conduct can be but one element in a personal bond that is more enduring"; what justification could there possibly be for denying the benefits of marriage to homosexual couples exercising "[t]he liberty protected by the Constitution"? Surely not the encouragement of procreation, since the sterile and the elderly are allowed to marry. This case "does not involve" the issue of homosexual marriage only if one entertains the belief that principle and logic have nothing to do with the decisions of this Court. Many will hope that, as the Court comfortingly assures us, this is so. (*Lawrence v. Texas*, 41 S. W. 3d 349, reversed and remanded [2003])

Heterosexual marriage "on shaky grounds"

[The Court's] reasoning leaves on pretty shaky grounds state laws limiting marriage to opposite-sex couples. Justice O'Connor seeks to preserve them by the conclusory statement that "preserving the traditional institution of marriage" is a legitimate state interest. But "preserving the traditional institution of marriage" is just a kinder way of describing the State's moral disapproval of same-sex couples. Texas's

interest … could be recast in similarly euphemistic terms: "preserving the traditional sexual mores of our society." In the jurisprudence Justice O'Connor has seemingly created, judges can validate laws by characterizing them as "preserving the traditions of society" (good); or invalidate them by characterizing them as "expressing moral disapproval" (bad)."
(*Lawrence v. Texas*, 41 S. W. 3d 349, reversed and remanded [2003])

CHAPTER 18

Supporting Community Decency

A judicial conservative works to uphold the right of communities to set public decency standards and resist the so-called right to indecent expression.

The First Amendment will lose none of its value to a free society if those who knowingly place themselves in the stream of pornographic commerce are obliged to make sure that they are not subsidizing child abuse. It is no more unconstitutional to make persons who knowingly deal in hard-core pornography criminally liable for the underage character of their entertainers than it is to make men who engage in consensual fornication criminally liable (in statutory rape) for the underage character of their partners.
Justice Antonin Scalia, *U.S. v. X-Citement Video*, 1994

"I believe very strongly in…the legitimacy of a government role in protecting traditional values."
Samuel Alito, 1985

*C*ommunities have throughout our history placed restrictions on sexu- ally oriented material to support community decency standards. This issue of public decency has been heightened in recent years by two factors: advances in communications technology and the Court's interest in expanding the First Amendment to include a right to indecency.

Numerous cases before the Supreme Court have challenged restrictions communities have placed upon sexually oriented material. Meanwhile, the courts are expanding "expression" rights to include even a funding requirement for indecent art. Justice Scalia argues that society has long restricted activity it deems inappropriate, and funding is not a require- ment of the First Amendment. The Scalia model upholds the constitu- tional right of communities to set decency standards while resisting the so-called right to indecency expression and its absurd funding mandate. Samuel Alito will have many opportunities to apply his judicial philoso- phy to this important issue. —S.E.

The Scalia Model on Supporting Community Decency

Constitution allows regulating morality

Our society prohibits, and all human societies have prohibited, certain activities not because they harm others but because they are considered, in the traditional phrase, "contra bonos mores," i.e., immoral. In American society, such prohibitions have included, for example, sadomasochism, cockfighting, bestiality, suicide, drug use, prostitution, and sodomy. While there may be great diversity of view on whether various of these prohibitions should exist (though I have found few ready to abandon, in principle, all of them) there is no doubt that, absent specific constitutional protection for the conduct involved, the Constitution does not prohibit them simply because they regulate "morality." (*Barnes v. Glen Theatre, Inc.*, 501 U.S. 560 [1991])

State may regulate conduct (such as public nudity)

I would uphold the Indiana statute on precisely the same ground: moral opposition to nudity supplies a rational basis for its prohibition, and since the First Amendment has no application to this case, no more than that is needed. Indiana may constitutionally enforce its prohibition of public nudity even against those who choose to use public nudity as a means of communication. The State is regulating conduct, not expression, and those who choose to employ conduct as a means of expression must make sure that the conduct they select is not generally forbidden. (*Barnes v. Glen Theatre, Inc.*, 501 U.S. 560 [1991])

Hardcore sex promoters have "no sanctuary in First Amendment"

Thus, a business that "(1) offer[s] ... hardcore sexual material, (2) as a constant and intentional objective of [its] business, [and] (3) seek[s] to promote it as such" finds no sanctuary in the First Amendment. ... It is not only children who can be protected from occasional uninvited exposure to what appellee calls "adult-oriented programming"; we can all be. ... In most contexts, contemporary American society has chosen to permit such commercial exploitation. That may be a wise democratic choice, if only because of the difficulty in many contexts (though not this one) of identifying the panderer to sex. It is, however, not a course compelled by the Constitution. Since the Government is entirely free to block these transmissions, it may certainly take the less drastic step of dictating how, and during what times, they may occur. (*U.S. v. Playboy Entertainment Group*, 529 U.S. 803 [2000])

No First Amendment right to subsidize child abuse

The First Amendment will lose none of its value to a free society if those who knowingly place themselves in the stream of pornographic commerce are obliged to make sure that they are not subsidizing child abuse. It is no more unconstitutional to make persons who knowingly deal in hard-core pornography criminally liable for the underage character of their entertainers than it is to make men who engage in consensual fornication criminally liable (in statutory rape) for the underage character of their partners. (*U.S. v. X-Citement Video*, 115 S. Ct. 464 [1994])

Funding obscene art — no constitutional mandate

The Court devotes so much of its opinion to explaining why this statute means something other than what it says that it neglects to cite the constitutional text governing our analysis. The First Amendment reads: "Congress shall make no law . . . abridging the freedom of speech." To abridge is "to contract, to diminish; to deprive of." With the enactment of §954(d)(1), Congress did not abridge the speech of those who disdain the beliefs and values of the American public, nor did it abridge indecent speech. Those who wish to create indecent and disrespectful art are as unconstrained now as they were before the enactment of this statute. Avant-garde artistes such as respondents remain entirely free to épater les bourgeois; they are merely deprived of the additional satisfaction of having the bourgeoisie taxed to pay for it. It is preposterous to equate the denial of taxpayer subsidy with measures "aimed at the suppression of dangerous ideas." (*National Endowment For Arts v. Finley*, 100 F.3d 671 [1998])

Government has discretion in art funding

One might contend, I suppose, that a threat of rejection by the only available source of free money would constitute coercion and hence "abridgment" within the meaning of the First Amendment. I would not agree with such a contention, which would make the [National Endowment for the Arts] the mandatory patron of all art too indecent, too disrespectful, or even too kitsch to attract private support. But even if one accepts the contention, it would have no application here. The NEA is far from the sole source of funding for art—even indecent, disrespectful, or just plain bad art. Accordingly, the Government may earmark NEA funds for projects it deems to be in the public interest without thereby abridging speech. (*National Endowment For Arts v. Finley*, 100 F.3d 671 [1998])

CHAPTER 19

Terrorism and War

*Chief Justice Scalia's understanding
of the constitutional jurisdiction of the courts
will not handcuff our military.*

For this Court to create such a monstrous scheme in time of war, and in frustration of our military commanders' reliance upon clearly stated prior law, is judicial adventurism of the worst sort. I dissent.
Justice Antonin Scalia, *Rasul v. Bush*, 2004

"The Supreme Court hit the doctrine of separation of powers about as hard as heavyweight champ Mike Tyson usually hits his opponents."
Samuel Alito, 1989, commenting on a Court decision upholding the independent counsel law.

---

*I*n 2004, the Supreme Court ruled in Rasul v. Bush *that rights of prisoners normally given to Americans also applied to prisoners of war held. The consequences of this Court ruling are far-reaching—placing the federal courts in the middle of our nation's ability to wage war in the 21st century and granting prisoners of war rights to sue in U.S. federal courts.*

Justice Scalia dissented in Rasul v. Bush, *arguing that this ruling marks an "unheralded expansion of federal court jurisdiction" and grants expansive rights to criminal aliens. In addition, Scalia argues that the Court should not involve itself in the waging of war by the executive branch of the government. Allowing every prisoner held during war to petition the courts creates a dangerous precedent. In the era of the War on Terror, we believe the Scalia model would help restore the constitutional bounds on the federal courts, allowing the executive branch to wage war under the auspices of Congress. —S.E.*

The Scalia Model on Terrorism and War

"Unheralded expansion of federal court jurisdiction"

The consequence of this holding, as applied to aliens outside the country, is breathtaking. It permits an alien captured in a foreign theater of active combat to bring a §2241 petition against the

Secretary of Defense. Over the course of the last century, the United States has held millions of alien prisoners abroad. A great many of these prisoners would no doubt have complained about the circumstances of their capture and the terms of their confinement. The military is currently detaining over 600 prisoners at Guantanamo Bay alone; each detainee undoubtedly has complaints — real or contrived — about those terms and circumstances. The Court's unheralded expansion of federal-court jurisdiction is not even mitigated by a comforting assurance that the legion of ensuing claims will be easily resolved on the merits. To the contrary, the Court says that the "[p]etitioners' allegations…unquestionably describe 'custody in violation of the Constitution or laws or treaties of the United States.'" From this point forward, federal courts will entertain petitions from these prisoners, and others like them around the world, challenging actions and events far away, and forcing the courts to oversee one aspect of the Executive's conduct of a foreign war. (*Rasul v. Bush*, 321 F.3d 1134, reversed and remanded [2004])

"Judicial adventuraism of the worst sort"

The Commander in Chief and his subordinates had every reason to expect that the internment of combatants at Guantanamo Bay would not have the consequence of bringing the cumbersome machinery of our domestic courts into military affairs. Congress is in session. If it wished to change federal judges' habeas jurisdiction from what this Court had previously held that to be, it could have done so. And it could have done so by intelligent revision of the statute, instead of by today's clumsy, countertextual reinterpretation that confers upon wartime prisoners greater habeas rights than domestic detainees. The latter must challenge their present physical confinement in the district of their confinement, whereas under today's strange holding Guantanamo Bay detainees can petition in any of the 94 federal judicial districts. The fact that extraterritorially located detainees lack the district of detention that the statute requires has been converted from a factor that precludes their ability to bring a petition at all into a factor that frees them to petition wherever they wish — and, as a result, to forum shop. For this Court to create such a monstrous scheme in time of war, and in frustration of our military commanders' reliance upon clearly stated prior law, is judicial adventurism of the worst sort. I dissent. (*Rasul v. Bush*, 321 F.3d 1134, reversed and remanded [2004])

Court gives criminal aliens more rights than non-criminal aliens

The Court today finds ambiguity in the utterly clear language of a statute that forbids the district court (and all other courts) to entertain the claims of aliens such as respondent St. Cyr, who have been found deportable by reason of their criminal acts. It fabricates a superclear statement, "magic words" requirement for the congressional expression of such an intent, unjustified in law and unparalleled in any other area of our jurisprudence. And as the fruit of its labors, it brings forth a version of the statute that affords criminal aliens more opportunities for delay-inducing judicial review than are afforded to non-criminal aliens, or even than were afforded to criminal aliens prior to this legislation concededly designed to expedite their removal. Because it is clear that the law deprives us of jurisdiction to entertain this suit, I respectfully dissent. (*INS v. St. Cyr*, 533 U.S. 289 [2001])

Wrongly extends rights to aliens overseas

The reality is this: Today's opinion, and today's opinion alone, overrules *Eisentrager*; today's opinion, and today's opinion alone, extends the habeas statute, for the first time, to aliens held beyond the sovereign territory of the United States and beyond the territorial jurisdiction of its courts. No reasons are given for this result; no acknowledgment of its consequences made. ... Today, the Court springs a trap on the Executive, subjecting Guantanamo Bay to the oversight of the federal courts even though it has never before been thought to be within their jurisdiction — and thus making it a foolish place to have housed alien wartime detainees. (*Rasul v. Bush*, 321 F.3d 1134, reversed and remanded [2004])

CHAPTER 20

America's Legal Sovereignty

Judicial conservatives must resist the encroachment of foreign laws and traditions in U.S. jurisprudence.

The basic premise of the Court's argument — that American law should conform to the laws of the rest of the world — ought to be rejected out of hand. In fact the Court itself does not believe it. In many significant respects the laws of most other countries differ from our law — including not only such explicit provisions of our Constitution as the right to jury trial and grand jury indictment, but even many interpretations of the Constitution prescribed by this Court itself.
Justice Antonin Scalia, January 13, 2005

"In my view, however, it makes no difference whether Canadian law is similar to or even in some sense better than ERISA [Employee Retirement Income Security Act]. What matters is that Congress wanted ERISA to govern the NHL pension plan, but the majority has frustrated the implementation of that intent."
Samuel Alito, *Dailey v. NHL*, 1993, dissent.

A disturbing trend has emerged in rulings by the Supreme Court of late. Rather than base decisions upon American law and the U.S. Constitution, the Court has introduced foreign sources for its decisions. These foreign sources have included selective references to world opinions, laws, and court decisions. This marks a dramatic turn in America's history of constitutional jurisprudence.

Justice Scalia argues that American law and tradition — ultimately rooted in the Constitution — should be the only standard that guides the Supreme Court. In Roper v. Simmons *he noted that the Court had made the opinions of U.S. citizens "irrelevant" in comparison to foreign authorities. This is a dangerous precedent that every judicial conservative must actively work to limit and correct. The Scalia model looks only to American sources. This is the unbending standard that Samuel Alito must uphold. —S.E.*

The Scalia Model on America's Legal Sovereignty

Court preferring international community over U.S. citizens

Though the views of our own citizens are essentially irrelevant to the Court's decision today, the views of other countries and the so-called international community take center stage. (*Roper v. Simmons*, 112 S. W. 3d 397, affirmed, [2005])

Court preferring other countries' laws over own states

It is interesting that whereas the Court is not content to accept what the States of our Federal Union say, but insists on inquiring into what they do (specifically, whether they in fact apply the juvenile death penalty that their laws allow), the Court is quite willing to believe that every foreign nation — of whatever tyrannical political makeup and with however subservient or incompetent a court system — in fact adheres to a rule of no death penalty for offenders under 18. (*Roper v. Simmons*, 112 S. W. 3d 397, affirmed, [2005])

Constitutional rights don't spring from foreign sources

Constitutional entitlements do not spring into existence because some States choose to lessen or eliminate criminal sanctions on certain behavior. Much less do they spring into existence, as the Court seems to believe, because foreign nations decriminalize conduct. (*Lawrence v. Texas*, 41 S. W. 3d 349, reversed and remanded [2003])

Reference to foreign law should be "rejected out of hand"

The basic premise of the Court's argument — that American law should conform to the laws of the rest of the world — ought to be rejected out of hand. In fact the Court itself does not believe it. In many significant respects the laws of most other countries differ from our law — including not only such explicit provisions of our Constitution as the right to jury trial and grand jury indictment, but even many interpretations of the Constitution prescribed by this Court itself. ... The Court should either profess its willingness to reconsider all ... matters in light of the views of foreigners, or else it should cease putting forth foreigners' views as part of the reasoned basis of its decisions. To invoke alien law when it agrees with one's own thinking, and ignore it otherwise, is not reasoned decisionmaking, but sophistry. ... What these foreign sources "affirm," rather than repudiate, is the Justices' own notion of how the world ought to be, and their diktat that it shall be so henceforth in America. The Court's parting attempt to downplay the significance of its extensive discussion of foreign law is unconvincing. "Acknowledgment" of foreign approval has no place in the legal opinion of this Court unless it is part of the basis for the Court's judgment — which is surely what it parades as today. (*Roper v. Simmons*, 112 S. W. 3d 397, affirmed, [2005])

Framers "would have been appalled"

We don't have the same moral and legal framework as the rest of the world, and never have. If you told the framers of the Constitution that [what] we're after is to... do something that will be just like Europe, they would have been appalled. And if you read the Federalist Papers, it's full of... statements that make very clear they didn't have a whole lot of respect for many of the rules in European countries. Madison, for example, speaks contemptuously of the countries on continental Europe "who are afraid to let their people bear arms." (Remarks at U.S. Association of Constitutional Law Discussion, Washington, DC, 1/13/05)

Why judges seek foreign references

But most of all, what does the opinion of a wise Zimbabwe judge or a wise member of the House of Lords law committee, what does that have to do with what Americans believe, unless you really think it's been given to YOU to make this moral judgment, a very difficult moral judgment? And so in making it for yourself and for the whole country, you consult whatever authorities you want. Unless you have that philosophy, I don't see how it's relevant at all. (Remarks at U.S. Association of Constitutional Law Discussion, Washington, DC, 1/13/05)

World community "irrelevant"

But the Prize for the Court's Most Feeble Effort to fabricate "national consensus" must go to its appeal (deservedly relegated to a footnote) to the views of assorted professional and religious organizations, members of the so-called "world community," and respondents to opinion polls. I agree with the Chief Justice, that the views of professional and religious organizations and the results of opinion polls are irrelevant. Equally irrelevant are the practices of the "world community," whose notions of justice are (thankfully) not always those of our people. We must never forget that it is a Constitution for the United States of America that we are expounding. ... [W]here there is not first a settled consensus among our own people, the views of other nations, however enlightened the Justices of this Court may think them to be, cannot be imposed upon Americans through the Constitution. (*Atkins v. Virginia*, 536 U.S. 304 [2002])

Selective use of foreign sources

That can't be the only explanation for not using other foreign sources, that we don't know what the other countries say. In my dissent in *Lawrence*, which was the homosexual sodomy case, I observed that the court cited only European law; said: Why, every European country has said you cannot prohibit homosexual sodomy. Of course, they said it not by some democratic ballot but by decree of the European Court of Human Rights, who was... using the same theory that we lawyers and judges and law students — we know what's moral and what isn't. It had not been done democratically. Nonetheless, it was true that throughout all of Europe, it was unlawful to prohibit homosexual sodomy. The court did not cite the rest of the world. It was easy to find out what the rest of the world thought about it. I cited in my dissent the rest of the world was equally divided. ... I mean, it lends itself to manipulation. It lends itself. It invites manipulation. You know, I want to do this thing; I have to think of some reason for it. ... I have to cite something. ... I have a decision by an intelligent man in Zimbabwe ... or anywhere else and you put it in there and you give the citation. By God, it looks lawyerly! And it lends itself to manipulation. It just does. (Remarks at U.S. Association of Constitutional Law Discussion, Washington, DC, 1/13/05)

CHAPTER 21

Judicial Confirmations and Independence

*Every American must stand for the principle of the
independent, non-politicized judiciary.*

The Bill of Rights is devised to protect you and me against, who do you think? The majority... The notion that the justices ought to be selected because of the positions that they will take, that are favored by the majority, is a recipe for destruction of what we have had for 200 years.

Justice Antonin Scalia, March 14, 2005

Related to the issue of separation of powers is the corruption of the judicial confirmation process. This corruption notably began with the confirmation process of Judge Robert Bork, a judge who had served with distinction for many years at the Circuit Court of Appeals. Strictly on the basis of Bork's perceived political views — i.e. the impact of his constitutional philosophy on contemporary political and legal questions – Bork's nomination was defeated. He was, as we now say, "Borked." The "lynching" of Clarence Thomas accelerated this process.

Today, federal court nominees are regularly blocked or defeated because of their perceived political views, not their legal qualifications. Again, this is a relatively new phenomenon in American history. For example, Antonin Scalia was confirmed 98-0 and Samuel Alito was unanimously confirmed to the Circuit Court of Appeals by a voice vote. Sen. Ted Kennedy said at the time that Alito had a "very distinguished record." Today a unanimous or near-unanimous vote for a judicial conservative is virtually an impossibility and many expect an "Armageddon" conflict before the final vote. Here are Scalia's sobering remarks on the politicizing of the judicial process. —S.E.

The Scalia Model on Judicial Confirmations and Independence

What has changed since Scalia's 98-0 confirmation

I was confirmed, close to 19 years ago now, by a vote of 98 to nothing. The two missing were Barry Goldwater and Jake Garnes, so make it 100. I was known at that time to be, in my political and social views, fairly conservative. But still, I was known to be a good lawyer, an honest man — somebody who could read a text and give it its fair meaning — had judicial impartiality and so forth. And so I was unanimously confirmed. Today, barely 20 years later, it is difficult to get someone confirmed to the Court of Appeals. What has happened? The American people have figured out what is going on. If we are selecting lawyers, if we are selecting people to read a text and give it the fair meaning it had when it was adopted, yes, the most important thing to do is to get a good lawyer. If, on the other hand, we're picking people to draw out of their own conscience and experience a new Constitution with all sorts of new values to govern our society, then we should not look principally for good lawyers. We should look principally for people who agree with us, the majority, as to whether there ought to be this right, that right, and the other right. We want to pick people that would write the new Constitution that we would want. (Remarks at the Woodrow Wilson Center, Washington, DC, 3/14/05)

What a call for "moderate" judges really means

And that is why you hear in the discourse on this subject people talking about moderate, we want moderate judges. What is a moderate interpretation of the text? Halfway between what it really means and what you'd like it to mean? There is no such thing as a moderate interpretation of the text. Would you ask a lawyer, "Draw me a moderate contract?" The only way the word has any meaning is if you are looking for someone to write a law, to write a constitution, rather than to interpret one. The moderate judge is the one who will devise the new constitution that most people would approve of. So, for example, we had a suicide case some terms ago, and the Court refused to hold that there is a constitutional right to assisted suicide. We said, "We're not yet ready to say that. Stay tuned, in a few years, the time may come, but we're not yet ready." And that was a moderate decision, because I think most people would not want — if we had gone, looked into that and created a national right to assisted suicide, that would have been an immoderate and extremist decision. (Remarks at the Woodrow Wilson Center, Washington, DC, 3/14/05)

Rendering the Constitution "useless"

I think the very terminology suggests where we have arrived — at the point of selecting people to write a constitution, rather than people to give us the fair meaning of one that has been democratically adopted. And when that happens, when the Senate interrogates nominees to the Supreme Court, or to the lower courts — you know, "Judge so-and-so, do you think there is a right to this in the Constitution? You don't? Well, my constituents think there ought to be, and I'm not going to appoint to the court someone who is not going to find that" — when we are in that mode, you realize, we have rendered the Constitution useless, because the Constitution will mean what the majority wants it to mean. The senators are representing the majority, and they will be selecting justices who will devise a constitution that the majority wants. And that, of course, deprives the Constitution of its principle utility. The Bill of Rights is devised to protect you and me against, who do you think? The majority.... The notion that the justices ought to be selected because of the positions that they will take, that are favored by the majority, is a recipe for destruction of what we have had for 200 years. (Remarks at the Woodrow Wilson Center, Washington, DC, 3/14/05)

APPENDIX

Judge Alito's Record:
Restraint, Commitment to Precedent,
Faithful Application of the Law*

1275 Pennsylvania Avenue, NW
Tenth Floor
Washington, DC 20004
www.committeeforjustice.org

* This report was produced by the Committee for Justice, including contributions by Executive Director Sean Rushton, General Counsel Curt Levey, and Research Director John Kalinger.

Executive Summary

With each Republican nominee to the Supreme Court – from Sandra Day O'Connor to John Roberts – attacks by liberal interest groups such as People for the American Way (PFAW) have become increasingly histrionic. Now the Left has trained its fire on Judge Samuel A. Alito, Jr. Despite the attacks, it would be difficult to imagine a candidate better suited to the High Court than Judge Alito. The son of an Italian immigrant and of two public-school teachers, Alito boasts an impeccable academic pedigree and has dedicated his career to public service, including fifteen years as a judge on the U.S. Court of Appeals for the Third Circuit. Notably, Judge Alito has more prior judicial experience than any Supreme Court nominee in the past 70 years.

As this report demonstrates, Judge Alito's record reveals him to be a thoughtful, restrained, and impartial jurist who avoids judicial policymaking. He decides the cases that come before him on the basis of the facts and the law – including precedent – without regard to his personal preferences on policy or outcome. While these characteristics are evident throughout Judge Alito's opinions, this report focuses on those issue areas where liberal interest groups have chosen to aim their attack, specifically:

Privacy: Judge Alito's record shows that he does not approach cases implicating privacy with a predetermined viewpoint. Instead, he decides such cases based on his understanding of what the law requires. On the issue of abortion rights, Alito voted on the pro-choice side in three of the four abortion cases in which he participated, and on the pro-life side in the fourth case. In other words, Judge Alito is neither a pro-life nor pro-choice judge, but a pro-law judge. And in a much-ballyhooed case involving the search of a 10-year old girl, the Left's only real complaint is that Alito declined to substitute his judgment for that of the police concerning the necessity of determining whether a drug dealer had hidden drugs on his daughter.

Constitutional Limits on Federal Power: In federalism cases, Judge Alito's fidelity to Supreme Court precedent and the Constitution's limits on federal power are being outrageously miscast as evidence that he opposes the federal ban on machine guns and the Family and Medical Leave Act.

Race and Sex Discrimination: Despite the Left's description of Alito's rulings on race and sex discrimination as "especially harsh," an examination of his record evinces a scholarly command of this complex area of the law, as well as an even-handed treatment of both plaintiffs and defendants.

Age and Disability Discrimination: Judge Alito is similarly even-handed in his consideration of age and disability discrimination claims. While that is not enough to satisfy critics of his record – who seem to believe that the disabled should win every case they bring – the truth is that Alito has decided many such cases in favor of disabled plaintiffs.

Other Labor and Employment Cases: Liberal special interest groups complain that Judge Alito's record in cases concerning "worker protection" is "mixed." What that really tells us is that Alito is not an outcome-oriented judge. In other words, he decides cases based on the facts and the law, not on what outcome he desires.

Religious Liberty: Judge Alito has struck down a variety of regulations that imposed unique burdens or outright restrictions on those wishing to express their religious views. Recognizing that the First Amendment's guarantee of religious liberty is not just for Christians, Alito has shown special sensitivity to the rights of religious minorities, such as Muslims and Native Americans.

Freedom of Speech: The "PC police" on the far Left sound the alarm because Judge Alito's opinions suggest "that student speech about morality and 'sin' should not be restricted even when it may offend others." But Judge Alito recognizes that protecting free speech even when others may disagree or be offended is precisely what the First Amendment is all about.

Prisoner Litigation: In a number of cases, Judge Alito has safeguarded the rights of prisoners – particularly inmates who claim that their convictions were tainted by racial discrimination. At the same time, Alito's record demonstrates that he grants appropriate deference to the judgment of officials charged with determining how best to run a prison.

Immigration Laws: Because they reflect his usual commitment to applying the law impartially, Judge Alito's opinions in this area fail to satisfy critics on the left who seem to think that every request for asylum should be granted. Never mind that Alito's application of the law has sometimes resulted in a broad view of eligibility for asylum and, in one case (*Fatin v. INS*), resulted in a legal rule that ensures that women who have suffered persecution abroad because of their gender or feminist beliefs will find a safe haven in the United States.

Distortion of Alito's Record

Despite Judge Alito's scholarly and evenhanded record across a wide variety of legal issues, liberal interest groups continue to try to portray him as out of the mainstream. That is no easy task, but here is how they do it. Like any impartial judge who hears hundreds of cases, there are numerous instances in which Alito has ruled against the type of parties favored by the Left – discrimination plaintiffs, aliens seeking asylum, prisoners, and the like. Similarly, there are numerous instances in which Alito has ruled in favor of such parties. Alito's critics on the left have taken advantage of this complex picture – conveniently ignoring the latter set of opinions, while reflexively attacking the former ones regardless of their legal reasoning – all in an effort to paint Alito as a judge who disfavors the "little guy."

The liberal interest groups arrayed against Judge Alito do not stop there. Even among the cherry-picked cases that they focus on, the Left chooses to ignore abundant evidence that Alito's legal analysis is well within the mainstream of American law. Examples of the types of evidence they overlook are:

- Alito's opinion spoke for a unanimous 3-judge panel or a lopsided full-circuit majority (in full report below, see, e.g., *Chittister, Keller, Hopp, Watson, Pemberthy, Poole, Saxe, Bolden, Sanguigni*).
- Democratic appointees on the Third Circuit agreed with Alito (see, e.g., *Chittister, Keller, Poole, Dia, Saxe, Schundler*).
- Other federal appeals courts agreed with Alito (see, e.g., *Chittister, Sheridan, Watson, Pemberthy, Rappa*).
- Alito's ruling was consistent with public opinion and the will of the public's elected representatives (see, e.g., *Casey*).

Alito's critics further distort the implications of his opinions by ignoring factors such as:

- The case turned on issues of a technical nature – such as burdens of proof, deadlines, complaint specificity, and warrant requirements – rather than on the substantive (and often emotional) issues Alito's critics point to (see, e.g., *McArdle, Bray, Sheridan, Poole, Groody*).
- Alito's opinion was based on the deference a federal appeals court must show to lower federal courts (*Bhaya, Glass*), state courts (*Pemberthy*), administrative law judges (*Grant, Chang, Dia*), and prison officials (*Banks, Fraise*).

Other Lines of Attack

Having failed to make any headway with the public through distortions of Judge Alito's substantive record, his critics are now trying to smear him with baseless ethics allegations. Specifically, they argue that Alito – who has money invested in Vanguard funds – should not have sat on a case in which a bankrupt party and her creditors were fighting over assets which had incidentally been held by Vanguard. However, a review of the facts and the governing federal ethics statutes, and an analysis by leading independent ethics experts, demonstrate that Judge Alito violated none of his ethical responsibilities. Moreover, as soon as Alito became aware of the possible conflict, he asked that the case be turned over to a new panel of judges.

The Left's assault on Alito has not been limited to his judicial record. His critics have gone so far as to attack statements he made in a 20 year old job application, five years before he became a judge. Most notably, they have pointed hysterically to his 1985 statement that he was "proud of [his] contributions in recent cases in which the government has argued . . . that the Constitution does not protect a right to an abortion."

This is much ado about nothing for a number of reasons. First of all, it is unreasonable to evaluate Judge Alito based on a decades-old statement rather than on his fifteen year record on the federal bench. That record – including ruling for the pro-choice side in three out of four cases – demonstrates that he puts his personal views aside when deciding cases. Moreover, the apparent basis for Alito's statement, a belief that *Roe v. Wade* was poorly reasoned, is widely held by legal scholars on both the right and the left. Finally, if expressing a view for or against a constitutional right to abortion were an appropriate bar to Supreme Court confirmation, Justices Stephen Breyer and Ruth Bader Ginsburg would not be on the Court today. Instead, both were overwhelming confirmed by the Senate despite having made their views on the issue clear.

Conclusion

This report demonstrates that, once again, the Left's attack on a Supreme Court nominee is based on distortion and hysterics, rather than on reality. The truth is that Judge Alito's judicial record reveals him to be an evenhanded, restrained, and thoughtful jurist who puts his personal preferences aside and leaves policymaking to the people's elected representatives in Congress and the states. Judge Alito will be a credit to the Supreme Court when he dons the judicial robe, and we call on the Senate to confirm him expeditiously.

For liberal interest groups such as People for the American Way (PFAW), the Alliance for Justice, and the Leadership Conference on Civil Rights, the Supreme Court was at its best in the 1960s and '70s when judicial activism was riding high.

Since then, the sky has been falling consistently for the liberal left. Starting with President Ronald Reagan, Republican-appointed federal judges have generally eschewed judicial activism and practiced constitutionalism and judicial restraint.

Fearing a non-political court that applies the law but does not legislate it, the liberal groups have poured their energy into attacking constitutionalist nominees to the federal appellate courts and the U.S. Supreme Court.

Now the Left has trained its fire on Judge Samuel A. Alito, Jr., the President's pick to sit on the Supreme Court.[1] Given the Left's previous distorted characterizations of Republican Supreme Court nominees, why should anyone believe their claims about Judge Alito now?

The fact is that it would be difficult to imagine a nominee better suited for the High Court than Judge Alito. The son of an Italian immigrant (and of two public-school teachers), Judge Alito has an impressive academic pedigree, with degrees from Princeton and Yale Law School. He had dedicated his career to public service, working as a federal prosecutor, a Justice Department official, and, for the past fifteen years, as a judge on the Philadelphia-based U.S. Court of

Appeals for the Third Circuit. In fact, he has more prior judicial experience than any Supreme Court nominee in the past 70 years.

Even more important is that Judge Alito's record reveals him to be a thoughtful, restrained jurist who shows an aversion to judicial policymaking. He decides the cases that come before him on the basis of the law and the facts, and leaves the legislating to the people's elected representatives in Congress and the States. Judge Alito will be a credit to the Supreme Court when he dons the judicial robe, and we call on the Senate to confirm him expeditiously.

A "Pro Law" Judge: Judge Alito's Privacy Record

Since Judge Alito does not engage in results oriented jurisprudence he does not decide cases "for privacy" or "against privacy"; he decides them based on his understanding of what the law requires. His willingness to follow the law wherever it leads explains why an independent analysis by the *Christian Science Monitor* found that, "of the four abortion cases in which he participated as an appeals court judge, he voted on the pro-choice side in all but one."[2] In other words, Judge Alito's "record is neither that of a 'pro-life' or 'pro-choice' judge, but of a 'pro-law' judge."[3]

One such "pro-law" ruling is Judge Alito's concurrence in *Planned Parenthood v. Farmer*, 220 F.3d 127 (3d Cir. 2000). In that opinion, Judge Alito agreed to strike down New Jersey's ban on partial-birth abortion. The Supreme Court previously had invalidated a similar Nebraska law, and Judge Alito emphasized the "responsibility" of judges "to follow and apply controlling Supreme Court precedent." This demonstrates that Judge Alito shows due deference to prior rulings of the Supreme Court notwithstanding his personal views, whatever they may be.

Judge Alito joined another "pro-law" opinion in *Elizabeth Blackwell Health Center for Women v. Knoll*, 61 F.3d 170 (3d Cir. 1995). That case presented a technical and arcane question of administrative law – whether administrative agencies are entitled to judicial deference when they adopt polices through informal means (like an opinion letter), as opposed to more formal notice-and-comment rule-making. Judge Alito concluded that agencies *are* entitled to deference in those circumstances. He therefore agreed that two Pennsylvania abortion regulations were preempted by the interpretation of the Hyde Amendment (a federal statute governing the availability of Medicaid funds to pay for abortions) announced by the Department of Health and Human Services. Once again, Judge Alito refused to use a case that indirectly dealt with abortion as a platform for imposing his views on the issue.

Of course, Exhibit A in the Left's bill of particulars is Judge Alito's partial dissent in *Planned Parenthood v. Casey*, 947 F.2d 682 (3d Cir. 1991). In that case, Judge Alito and his Third Circuit colleagues – and later the Supreme Court – agreed that three of the four Pennsylvania laws at issue in that case were perfectly constitutional. Specifically, the appellate court unanimously held that states can: (1) require that information be given to women considering abortion to enable them to make an informed choice; (2) prevent minor girls from having abortions unless a parent approves; and (3) oblige abortion providers to publicly report certain non-confidential information. Each of these holdings was upheld by the Supreme Court.

The only issue on which Judge Alito parted company from his colleagues was the permissibility of a law requiring that, unless one of several exceptions applied, a married woman seeking an abortion had to sign a form indicating that she informed her spouse. (Note that the law didn't require the woman to get her spouse's *permission*. Nor did the law require her to actually notify her spouse; she simply had to sign a form stating that she had done so.) Judge Alito engaged in a lengthy analysis of Justice O'Connor's prior abortion-related writings and by applying existing precedent sustained the spousal-notification requirement. Ultimately, a majority on the Supreme Court disagreed, and the law was invalidated. But there can be no doubt about Judge Alito's good-faith effort to scrupulously apply the High Court's past decisions.

It goes without saying that spousal-notification laws like Pennsylvania's enjoy wide popularity among the American people. When Gallup in 1992 – the same year the Supreme Court handed down its *Casey* decision – "asked people whether they favored or opposed a law requiring that the husband of a married woman be notified if she decides to have an abortion, 73 percent said they were in favor." Levels of support have remained stratospheric ever since. "In 1996, 70 percent were in favor, and in 2003, 72 percent were." Only about a quarter of Americans oppose such laws.[4]

The spousal-notification requirement also commanded strong bipartisan support from Pennsylvania lawmakers. Signed into law by a Democratic governor in 1989, the legislation (Senate Bill 369) passed the Democrat-controlled House by an impressive 143-58 margin, including 67 of the chamber's 101 Democrats. The vote in the Senate was similarly lopsided: 33-17, including a majority of the Democrats. If Judge Alito is unfit for the Supreme Court because he concluded that spousal-notification laws pass constitutional muster, then three-quarters of the American people are too extreme for the Left's taste. Who's the radical here?

Predictably, much has been made of then Assistant Solicitor General Alito's comments in a 1985 job application to be Deputy Assistant Attorney General that he was "proud of [his] contributions in recent cases in which the government has argued...that the Constitution does not protect a right to an abortion." However, the media reports and left-wing accusations are much ado about nothing.

First, the application was written just twelve years after *Roe*, before the Supreme Court's *Casey v. Planned Parenthood* decision affirmed that there is a constitutional right to abortion. Judge Alito has shown himself to be a judge who gives *stare decisis* its full and proper respect.

The last twenty years of Supreme Court precedent will surely factor into his reasoning as a Supreme Court justice.

Second, as discussed above, there is no indication that his judicial opinions have reflected any personal views he may have concerning abortion. Instead, he has made every attempt to follow Justice O'Connor's "undue burden" standard, including ruling against what would have to be considered the "pro-life" position in *Planned Parenthood v. Farmer* and *Blackwell Health*. When it comes to privacy, Judge Alito's record is clearly one of modesty and judicial restraint, not that of an activist who imposes his own policy preferences on the law.

Third, it would be unreasonable to evaluate Judge Alito based on a twenty year old statement rather than his fifteen year record on the federal bench, during which time he has written many hundreds of opinions. It is by that record as a *judge*, rather than by a job application written in 1985, that his judicial philosophy and temperament should be measured. Before being nominated to the High Court, Justice Ruth Bader Ginsburg had advocated some views that would be considered by many to be out of the "mainstream," such as the abolition of Mother's and Father's Days, co-ed prisons, and a constitutional right to prostitution and polygamy.[5] However, the Senate properly evaluated her nomination based on her extensive record as a judge, not her previous record as an advocate.

Fourth, Judge Alito's criticism of the view that abortion is a constitutional right should not be a bar to his confirmation, just as comments supporting the right to abortion were not a bar to the confirmation of Justices Stephen Breyer and Ginsburg, both of whom received an overwhelming majority of votes in the Senate. The Senate should uphold the same standard for both Republican and Democratic nominees to the Court and not impose a litmus test – especially a one-sided test – on abortion or any other issue.

Finally, the idea that *Roe v. Wade* was poorly reasoned is widely held by legal scholars and judges both on the right and the left. Liberal law professors such as Laurence Tribe, Cass Sunstein, and Alan Dershowitz have been critical of *Roe* as an example of judicial activism and overreach.[6] Indeed, even Justice Ginsburg, in a law review article in 1985 – the same year as Judge Alito's application – stated that Roe's "[h]eavy handed judicial intervention was difficult to justify and appears to have provoked, not resolved, conflict."[7]

By now it should come as no surprise that left-wing groups' characterization of Judge Alito's dissent in *Doe v. Groody*, 361 F.3d 232 (3d Cir. 2004), a case involving a search for illegal drugs, is a gross distortion. In *Doe*, police officers obtained from a judge a warrant to search John Doe's residence for drug paraphernalia. The accompanying warrant application sought permission to search all occupants of the house – on the reasonable theory that drug dealers often secret their wares on others' persons in order to evade detection. However, the warrant's description of the persons and places to be searched only listed John Doe and his residence, apparently because the box on the form was too small to fit the rest of the information. When executing the warrant, a female officer took Jane and Mary Doe (John Doe's wife and 10-year-old daughter, respectively) to a private room and searched them for drugs, asking them to shift or remove various articles of clothing. This is hardly the invasive "strip-search" that PFAW bewails.

The issue in *Doe* had nothing to do with whether the wife and daughter could be strip-searched. The fact that the search involved a female police officer asking Jane and Mary Doe to adjust their clothes simply was not relevant to the outcome of the case. Instead, the issue was a mundane and technical question of criminal law: How precisely must a search warrant incorporate the terms of an accompanying application?

Disagreeing with his colleagues' decision to invalidate the search, Judge Alito paid heed to the Supreme Court's instructions that applications for search warrants must be read "in a commonsense and realistic fashion." *United States v. Ventresca*, 380 U.S. 102, 108 (1965).

His basic point was that the warrant should not be interpreted in a "technical and legalistic" way. The police officers in their application specifically indicated that they intended to search all occupants of the Doe residence. The only reason they didn't repeat that request in the search warrant itself was because the relevant box on the warrant was not large enough.

In the end, PFAW's complaint about *Groody* amounts to this: Judge Alito did not impose on the police a judge-created policy that it is better not to search the children of drug dealers, a policy that may well result in dealers having carte blanche to use their children as mules. Only one determined to close his eyes to reality – like PFAW – could regard *Doe* as evidence that Judge Alito favors strip-searches of ten-year-olds. If anything, *Doe* demonstrates that Judge Alito is not hidebound to hyper-technical, literalist methods of interpreting legal texts.

A Strong But Not Omnipotent Federal Government

Liberals' distortions of Judge Alito's dissent in *United States v. Rybar*, 103 F.3d 273 (3d Cir. 1996), are tendentious and misleading in the extreme. First, *Rybar* was not a "gun control" case. Nor, despite defendant Rybar's game attempt to make it so, was it a Second Amendment case. *Rybar* centered on the scope of Congress's power under the Constitution's Commerce Clause.

At the time the Third Circuit heard *Rybar*, the Supreme Court in the *Lopez* case had indicated that Congress's Commerce Clause power, though broad, was not without its limits. Judge Alito noted that while the majority wanted to strictly limit *Lopez* to "its own peculiar circumstances," the court had a "responsibility to apply Supreme Court precedent." It is improper to draw any conclusion from *Rybar* as to what Judge Alito's position, whether personal or legal, on gun control might be. For example, Judge Alito pointed out that even if the federal statute in question was struck down, that "would not preclude adequate regulation of the private possession of machine guns.

Needless to say, the Commerce Clause does not prevent the states from regulating machine gun possession, as all of the jurisdictions within our circuit have done."

Judge Alito's *Rybar* dissent also emphasized that federal courts are not supposed to be the taskmaster of Congress. He specifically wrote that, "[o]f course, Congress is not obligated to make findings" of fact for a piece of legislation to be sustained. He did, however, follow the Supreme Court's guidance in *Lopez*, which held that congressional factual findings would have been helpful in aiding the Court's evaluation of Congress's authority to enact the statute in question. In other words, Judge Alito was doing no more than faithfully seeking to apply governing precedent from the Supreme Court. He also properly noted that Congress never even bothered to identify the source of its constitutional authority to enact the statute challenged in *Rybar*.

In addition to suggesting that congressional findings could have saved the statute, Judge Alito also indicated that Congress could have shored-up the law's constitutionality by adding a jurisdictional element – i.e., making plain that Congress was only seeking to regulate those firearms-related activities that impact interstate commerce. Judge Alito emphasized that a jurisdictional element is "a common feature of federal laws in this field and one that has not posed any noticeable problems for federal law enforcement." He also correctly noted that the lack of a jurisdictional element was one of the reasons why the Supreme Court in *Lopez* struck down the law as unconstitutional. These are the hallmarks of a fair-minded judge.

The Left's distortions of *Chittister v. Department of Community & Economic Development*, 226 F.3d 223 (3d Cir. 2000), suffers from equally fatal flaws. In that case, a unanimous panel of the Third Circuit voted to strike down portions of the Family Medical Leave Act ("FMLA") as an unconstitutional abrogation of the immunity from lawsuits which states enjoy under the Eleventh Amendment. It bears emphasis that Judge Alito was the only Republican-appointed judge on the three-member panel. He was joined by Judge McKee (a Clinton appointee) and Judge Fullam (a Johnson appointee), both of whom agreed that the relevant parts of the statute were unconstitutional.

That Judge Alito was joined by two Democrats is powerful evidence that he was doing no more than seeking to apply the Supreme Court's recent pronouncements in this area of law. At the time *Chittister* was decided, the High Court had decided a number of cases, stretching back over a century, indicating that Congress does not enjoy an unchecked power to abrogate the states' sovereign immunity. *See, e.g., Hans v. Louisiana,* 134 U.S. 1 (1890); *Seminole Tribe v. Florida,* 517 U.S. 44 (1996); *City of Boerne v. Flores,* 521 U.S. 507 (1997); *Florida Prepaid v. College Savings Bank,* 527 U.S. 627 (1999); *Alden v. Maine,* 527 U.S. 706 (1999); *Kimel v. Florida Board of Regents,* 528 U.S. 62 (2000); *University of Alabama v. Garrett,* 531 U.S. 356 (2001). In each case, the Court held that Congress improperly attempted to abrogate the states' Eleventh Amendment sovereign immunity.

The Third Circuit was far from the only federal court to interpret these precedents as casting doubt on the constitutionality of the FMLA. Indeed, a number of circuits from around the country – including the First, Second, Fourth, Fifth, Sixth, and Eighth Circuits – held that the FMLA did not abrogate the states' Eleventh Amendment immunity. *See Laro v. New Hampshire,* 259 F.3d 1 (1st Cir. 2001); *Hale v. Mann,* 219 F.3d 61 (2d Cir. 2000); *Montgomery v. Maryland,* 266 F.3d 334 (4th Cir. 2001); *Kazmier v. Widmann,* 225 F.3d 519 (5th Cir. 2000); *Sims v. University of Cincinnati,* 219 F.3d 559 (6th Cir. 2000); *Townsel v. Missouri,* 233 F.3d 1094 (8th Cir. 2000).

To be sure, the Supreme Court in *Nevada Department of Human Resources v. Hibbs,* 538 U.S. 721 (2003), later ruled that a different section of the FMLA did represent a valid abrogation of the states' Eleventh Amendment immunity. However, *Hibbs* is plainly distinguishable from *Chittister,* as the Supreme Court and several courts of appeals have recognized. (*Chittister* dealt with a worker's right under the FMLA to take sick leave for him- or herself; *Hibbs* dealt with a worker's right to take leave to have a child or care for family members. Because women often exercise the latter set of rights, and because Congress has the power to combat gender-based stereotypes, the Supreme Court in *Hibbs* employed a more generous standard of review than would apply in ordinary FMLA cases like *Chittister*.) The fact that so many federal judges agreed with Judge Alito – including countless Democratic appointees – demonstrates that his ruling fits comfortably within the mainstream of American law.

Scholarly and Equitable Consideration of Race and Sex Discrimination Claims

Judge Alito's opinions applying civil rights and non-discrimination statutes evince a scholarly command of this complex area of law and an even-handed treatment of both plaintiffs and defendants. Virtually all of his rulings are consistent with holdings of other federal appellate courts, showing his interpretations to be well within the mainstream of the federal bench. Most importantly, Judge Alito's analysis consistently displays a careful fidelity to the statutory text, congressional intent, and governing Supreme Court precedent.

Judge Alito's sensitivity to the issue of discrimination – in particular, gender-based discrimination – is evidenced in *Fatin v. INS*, 12 F.3d 1233 (3d Cir. 1993). In that case, an Iranian woman petitioned for asylum. Writing for the court, Judge Alito ruled that a woman would be entitled to asylum in the United States if she introduced sufficient evidence that compliance with Iran's "gender specific laws and repressive social norms" – such as the requirement that women wear a veil in public – would be deeply abhorrent to her. Judge Alito also indicated that asylum would be available to a woman who could show that she would be persecuted in her home country because of her gender, because of her commitment to feminism, or because of her membership in a feminist group. The court ultimately concluded that the woman in that particular case had not introduced enough evidence to establish that she had a well-founded fear of persecution, and that she therefore was not entitled to asylum. But the legal rule Judge Alito articulated in *Fatin* ensures that women who show they have suffered persecution on account of their gender or feminist beliefs will find a safe haven in the United States.

Judge Alito's rulings in civil rights cases have been breathlessly described by those on the Left as "especially harsh." But this overblown rhetoric is betrayed by even a cursory examination of the Judge Alito's record. The Left's apparent strategy is to mischaracterize and distort Judge Alito's record in the hopes that its readers are too lazy to examine the cases for themselves.

For example, in their preliminary report on Judge Alito PFAW singles out his dissent in *Glass v. Philadelphia Elect. Co.*, 34 F.3d 188 (3d Cir. 1994), as somehow reflecting a less-than-sterling commitment to civil-rights laws. In reality, the case involved a technical question of appellate review – did the "abuse of discretion" standard that applies when an appellate court reviews certain lower court rulings require the Third Circuit to uphold a disputed evidentiary ruling by the district court? Judge Alito concluded that the trial court's ruling should be sustained. There's nothing radical about this concept; the notion that trial courts' evidentiary rulings are entitled to special deference on appellate review has been a cardinal principle of the American legal system for centuries.

Another case that has been distorted is *Watson v. SEPTA*, 207 F.3d 207 (3d Cir. 2000). Here, writing for a unanimous panel, Judge Alito upheld a jury verdict in an employment discrimination case, finding that the lower court did not commit reversible error when giving instructions to the jury. It bears noting that Judge Alito's opinion simply followed the interpretation announced by the only two circuits to have previously considered the issue. And his opinion drew heavily on a prior concurrence by Justice O'Connor, which Congress subsequently ratified in a later amendment to Title VII.

The next case in the parade of horribles is *Sheridan v. E.I. DuPont de Nemours and Co.*, 100 F.3d 1061 (3d Cir. 1996) (en banc), in which Judge Alito dissented from an *en banc* decision of the Third Circuit. The *Sheridan* decision turned on a difficult question that had split the circuits and that involved the complex burden-shifting scheme of presumptions and inferences that courts apply in determining whether a Title VII claim should go to trial. Judge Alito simply interpreted the Supreme Court's much-disputed language in a previous case as requiring that a Title VII plaintiff who makes a specified (and a relatively low) showing should "usually" – but not necessarily "always" – be permitted to go to trial. Judge Alito's dissent noted that "[i]f the majority had merely said that, under the circumstances described above, a defense motion for summary judgment or judgment as a matter of law must generally be denied, I would agree," but he found the "blanket rule" adopted by the majority to be legally "unsound." Judge Alito was far from the only circuit court judge to reach that conclusion – the same outcome also was reached by unanimous panels of the First and Eleventh Circuits, and by 16 out of 17 Fifth Circuit judges sitting *en banc*. Finally, four years later, in an opinion written by Justice O'Connor, a unanimous Supreme Court agreed with Judge Alito's position in *Reeves v. Sanderson Plumbing Products, Inc.*, 150 U.S. 133 (2000).

Liberal special interest groups and politicians seem particularly incensed by Judge Alito's dissent in *Bray v. Marriott Hotels*, 110 F.3d 986 (3d Cir. 1997), but what they do not understand is that what divides Judge Alito from the majority in this case is Judge Alito's belief that claims of discrimination require evidence of actual discrimination and not an employer's mere non-compliance with its own internal procedures. Bray, an African-American female and a Marriott employee, had applied for a promotion, along with several other hotel employees. Marriott instead offered the position to Riehle, a white female. Bray sued under Title VII, claiming that she had been denied the promotion because of her race. The district court had granted summary judgment to Marriott, finding that Bray not had offered enough evidence to either (1) cast doubt on the reasons offered by Marriott for promoting Riehle over Bray ("Prong One"), or (2)allow the jury to infer that discrimination was likely a motivating cause of the promotion decision ("Prong Two"). Marriott explained that it selected Riehle because she was the best applicant for the position. Compared to Bray, Riehle's qualifications were clearly superior, including a higher objective rating, greater experience, and participation in more seminars and training sessions.

The panel majority found that the facts were sufficiently in dispute that the district court's decision to grant summary judgment for Marriott was improper. Judge Alito, in dissent, first made clear that he understood Bray to be challenging the district court's ruling only on Prong One. He explained (quoting Third Circuit case law) that Prong One "requires that plaintiff point to evidence from which a reasonable factfinder can 'disbelieve the employer's articulated reasons'" (rather than merely disagree with them). He then described in detail how Bray had failed to satisfy her burden under Prong One. In its preliminary report PFAW asserts that Alito's dissent "made clear that he would have imposed an almost impossible evidentiary burden on victims of employment discrimination," but that distortion has no basis in reality. In particular, PFAW appears not to understand that Judge Alito's departure from the majority related only to the plaintiff's evidentiary burden under Prong One – and only then involved a small, and nuanced, difference in interpretation of the Supreme Court's governing (and ambiguous) pronouncements regarding how this burden was to be met.

Nothing about Judge Alito's opinion for a unanimous court in *Hopp v. Pittsburgh*, 194 F.3d 434 (3d Cir. 1999), reveals any hostility to affirmative action programs. In that case, the city of Pittsburgh revised its procedures for hiring police officers. The new policy supplemented the city's traditional written test – which some feared would disadvantage African-American applicants – with an oral test. Several white police officers were deemed to have failed their oral tests and they sued, arguing that they were victims of race-based discrimination. After trial, the jury found in the white officers' favor, and the Third Circuit unanimously affirmed the verdict.

Hopp tells us nothing about Judge Alito's inclinations one way or the other with respect to affirmative action. Rather, the case involved the straightforward application of principles of antidiscrimination law that have been settled since the Supreme Court's ruling in *McDonnell Douglas Corp. v. Green*, 411 U.S. 792 (1973). *Hopp* was a run-of-the-mill case in which the plaintiffs presented their evidence that they had suffered discrimination, the city presented its evidence that discrimination was not the reason the white officers weren't hired, and the jury after weighing all available evidence decided in favor of the plaintiffs.

Some of the plaintiffs' evidence – which the jury found more persuasive than the city's evidence – included the following: (1) the city's prior written examination was not biased and was a powerful predictor of job performance; (2) the city refused to explain why any of the plaintiffs failed the oral examination; (3) the city initially planned to fail 15% of the applicants who made it to the oral examination phase, but then raised that number to 35% in an attempt to hire fewer white applicants; (4) the city undercut 29 white applicants who passed all of their examinations, but did not undercut any similarly-situated African-American applicants; and (5) while the city failed many white applicants who performed well on the written examination, it failed very few African-Americans who performed poorly on the written examination.

Sensitivity to Age and Disability Discrimination

Given the enormous number of employment discrimination cases that come before the federal courts, it is unsurprising that any federal judge will have issued decisions ruling both for and against plaintiffs claiming age discrimination. Judge Alito's record is entirely typical. In *Showalter v. University of Pittsburgh Medical Center*, 190 F.3d 231 (1999), for example, he found in favor of the employee and reversed a grant of summary judgment for the Medical Center. Showalter had been terminated as part of a reduction-in-force ("RIF"), which the Medical Center claimed has been based on department seniority. The Magistrate Judge applied older Third Circuit law governing RIF cases and found that Showalter could not prove age discrimination because he could not show that Medical Center had retained an "unprotected worker." Judge Alito concluded his was the wrong legal standard. He looked to more recent non-RIF cases in which the employee had to show only that the employer had been replaced by someone "sufficiently younger," and he extended those precedents to apply to RIF cases. On that basis, Judge Alito found in favor of Showalter.

Judge Alito also reversed the lower court's determination that no reasonable factfinder could have rejected the Medical Center's proffered nondiscriminatory reason for terminating Showalter – that he had the least departmental seniority. Judge Alito carefully reviewed the record evidence and found that the Medical Center did not automatically make RIF decisions based on *departmental* seniority; in some cases, they relied on seniority in a particular job or seniority at a particular hospital. According to Judge Alito, a reasonable factfinder could have concluded that the Medical Center chose to use departmental seniority so it could discriminate against Showalter. He therefore reversed the lower court's decision and allowed Showalter to continue his action against the Medical Center.

Of course, Judge Alito's careful evaluations of legal standards and record evidence mean little to the far Left, which seems to believe that employees should win every case of employment discrimination they bring. Thus, PFAW complains about Judge Alito's decision in *Bhaya v. Westinghouse Electric Corporation*, 922 F.2d 184 (1990). Judge Alito wrote for a panel majority that rejected the plaintiffs' technical evidentiary challenges to a district court's decision against them. As any appellate lawyer knows, such evidentiary challenges rarely succeed because the trial court is entitled to significant deference on factual and evidentiary issues. Indeed, the panel majority concluded that most of the plaintiffs' claims "clearly lack[ed] merit."

PFAW also distorts Judge Alito's record in its criticism of the majority opinion in *Grant v. Shalala*, 989 F.2d 1332 (3d Cir. 1993). In that case, the Third Circuit ruled that the district court lacked authority to conduct its own factfinding to determine whether an administrative law judge (ALJ) was biased, and that the district court's role was limited to reviewing the agency's findings on the issue. Judge Alito's opinion, emphasizing the importance of safeguarding the impartiality of agency adjudications, found that the statutorily-mandated course for a claimant wishing to challenge an ALJ's impartiality was to pursue first disqualification of the ALJ, then administrative appeal, and finally judicial review. PFAW's criticisms make plain that its real complaint against Judge Alito is that, in the process of faithfully applying governing law and requiring adherence to process, he does not invariably reach PFAW's preferred result.

Criticism of *Keller v. Orix Credit Alliance*, 130 F.3d 1101 (3d Cir. 1997) (en banc), is even more unfounded. In that case, Keller sued his former employer for age discrimination, when he had been discharged following his complete failure to even come close to raising capital that was essential to the business. Although Keller claimed he was discriminated against on account of his age, his employer replaced him with someone who was not even five years younger than Keller. Judge Alito's decision for the en banc Third Circuit was joined by eight of his eleven colleagues – including an appointee of President Carter and an appointee of President Clinton.

Another supposed example Judge Alito's insensitivity to the elderly and disabled is his decision in *McArdle v. Tronetti*, 961 F.2d 1083 (3d

Cir. 1992). Judge Alito receives complaints from the Left for requiring the discrimination claim in that case be pled with specificity, even though a later (and entirely unrelated) Supreme Court case held that such specificity was not required. The requirement that certain discrimination claims be pled with specificity was the law of the Third Circuit, settled by a precedent that pre-dated Judge Alito's tenure on the bench. *See Colburn v. Upper Darby Township*, 838 F.2d 663, 666 (3d Cir. 1988). Thus, Judge Alito did nothing more than correctly apply the mandatory precedents of the Third Circuit. Not only was Judge Alito following the binding precedents of the Third Circuit, but the Third Circuit was not the only court at the time that required a heightened pleading standard for such claims. The Supreme Court recognized this fact in a later case, when it resolved the circuit split over the specificity with which discrimination claims must be pled. *See Leatherman v. Tarrant County Narcotics Intelligence & Coordination Unit*, 507 U.S. 163, 165 (1993) (citing cases on both sides of circuit split).

This same evenhandedness is also on display in Judge Alito's disability-discrimination cases, many of which have been decided in favor of disabled plaintiffs. For example, in *Polini v. Lucent Technologies*, 100 Fed. Appx. 112 (3d Cir. 2004), Judge Alito held in favor of a plaintiff whose former employer refused to rehire her, purportedly because her eyesight was so poor that it made it impossible for her to resume her former position as a detailer. Judge Alito ruled that the plaintiff had introduced enough evidence that her case should have been allowed to go before a jury, rather than being disposed of by summary judgment. In another recent opinion, *Shapiro v. Township of Lakewood*, 292 F.3d 356 (3d Cir. 2002), Judge Alito reversed the district court's grant of summary judgment against a disabled employee simply because the employee had not complied with the employer's policy regarding transfer applications. Judge Alito returned the case to the district court with instructions to allow the employee, consistent with governing Supreme Court precedent, the opportunity to demonstrate that the employer could have provided reasonable accommodation of his disability.

Left-wing groups also criticize three other opinions by Judge Alito that did not come out fully in favor of the disabled plaintiffs. For example, *Caruso v. Blockbuster-Sony Music Entertainment Center*, 193 F.3d 730 (3d Cir. 1999), required the court to interpret two Justice Department regulations as they pertained to wheelchair-user sight lines and access to certain recreational facilities. Writing for a unanimous panel, Judge Alito ruled *in favor* of the disabled litigants on one of the two questions. Specifically, he reversed the district court's ruling that the defendant need not make the lawn area of a concert venue wheelchair-accessible given that there were numerous closer (and thus "better") seats that were wheelchair accessible. Judge Alito wrote that such a justification is "repugnant to the [Americans with Disabilities Act]" and "treats the ADA's requirement of equal access for people with disabilities as a 'particular technical and scoping requirement.' This is simply not the case. Rather, equal access is an explicit requirement of both the statute itself and the general provisions of the DOJ's regulations." On the other question, Judge Alito engaged in an in-depth analysis of the relevant rule's ambiguous history and meaning before concluding that it required the provision of dispersed wheelchair locations offering a variety of sight lines comparable to the variety of sight lines available to the general public. This ultimately was a *broader* reading than the alternate interpretation urged by the disabled appellants – namely, a requirement that such venues provide sight lines over standing spectators if such sight lines were available to the general public.

Equally baffling are objections to two other disability-related opinions. In one, *Ford v. Schering-Plough Corp.*, 145 F.3d 601 (3d Cir. 1998), Judge Alito concurred with the majority's conclusion that the plaintiff had failed to state a claim because the ADA does not prohibit bona fide insurance plans from providing different coverage for different disabilities. He parted company with the majority merely because he believed that this conclusion – that the plaintiff had failed to state a claim – was all that was necessary to dispose of the case and that the majority unnecessarily reached the remaining issues. In another partial concurrence/partial dissent in *Nathanson v. Medical College of Pennsylvania*, 926 F.2d 1368 (3d Cir. 1991), Judge Alito simply took the position, based on a factual record very damaging to the plaintiff, that a student who had left medical school a week into classes had not given the school ample notice of her need for special disability-related accommodations.

Fair-Minded in Other Labor and Employment Cases

Some on the Left have asserted that Judge Alito's record in cases concerning "worker protection" is somehow "mixed." Yet the two cases cited for that proposition demonstrate quite the opposite – that Judge Alito is both fair and well within the mainstream. In *Bolden v. Southeastern Pennsylvania Transportation Authority*, 953 F.2d 807 (3d Cir. 1991) (en banc), Judge Alito wrote for an overwhelming 7-3 majority of the judges on the Third Circuit. Far from granting the employer a free pass, he rejected most of its arguments. But he found that where a union had agreed that employees would participate in drug tests, a worker's failure to take the union-approved test was grounds for discharge. And in *Mitchum v. Hurt*, 73 F.3d 30 (3d Cir. 1995), Judge Alito issued an unabashedly pro-worker opinion that allowed federal employees to bring claims in federal court even when they had not pursued remedies before an administrative agency. He went further than most federal appeals courts in holding that workers could seek equitable remedies such as reinstatement.

A Commitment to Religious Liberty

In case after case, Judge Alito has given effect to the First Amendment's guarantees of religious liberty. He has struck down a host of regulations that impose unique burdens or outright restrictions on those who wish to express their religious views, and he has shown special sensitivity to the rights of religious minorities. Judge Alito also has refused to sanction the efforts of radical secularists to purge the public square of all references to religion. Even PFAW has conceded, as it must, that Judge Alito "defend[s] the asserted rights of individuals to freely exercise their faith."

Time and again, Judge Alito has resisted government efforts to discriminate against people of faith. In *Child Evangelism Fellowship v. Stafford Township School District*, 386 F.3d 514 (3d Cir. 2004), he invalidated a school policy that allowed various student groups to distribute informational materials, but that barred a religious organization from doing the same. According to the court, "Stafford disfavored Child Evangelism because of the particular religious views that Child Evangelism espouses." In fact, during the proceedings, the school "sought to elicit Child Evangelism's admission that it adheres to a variety of traditional Christian doctrines"; the school's lawyer described those doctrines as "inconsistent with what we're obligated to teach, that being diversity and tolerance." Judge Alito thus saw the school's rule for what it was: a classic case of viewpoint discrimination.

Another example of Judge Alito's commitment to the First Amendment is *C.H. v. Oliva*, 226 F.3d 198 (3d Cir. 2000) (en banc). There, the majority upheld a school's decision to remove a student's religious poster from a Thanksgiving holiday display, and to bar the student from reading a religious-themed story to his class. (Other students were permitted to display secular posters and to read secular stories.) Judge Alito dissented, arguing that "public school students have the right to express religious views in class discussion or in assigned work." In particular, "the poster was allegedly given discriminatory treatment because of the viewpoint that it expressed, because it expressed thanks for Jesus, rather than for some secular thing. This was quintessential viewpoint discrimination, and it was proscribed by the First Amendment."

Judge Alito properly recognizes that the First Amendment's guarantee of religious liberty is not just for Christians. Rather, the constitutional right to worship according to the dictates of one's conscience is the birthright of every American, regardless of faith. In *Blackhawk v. Pennsylvania*, 381 F.3d 202 (3d Cir. 2004), Judge Alito struck down a state law that required keepers of wild animals to obtain a permit, and that contained no exemption for those who sought to keep such animals for religious purposes. The plaintiff was a Native American who wanted to keep wild bears, which his faith regards as sacred. Similarly, in *Fraternal Order of Police Newark Lodge No. 12 v. City of Newark*, 170 F.3d 359 (3d Cir. 1999), Judge Alito invalidated a rule that required police officers to shave their beards, and that contained no religious exemption. The plaintiffs were Sunni Muslims who believed they had a religious duty to grow beards.

Despite Judge Alito's record of protecting religious liberty, the Left will always find something to complain about. For example, in their preliminary report on Judge Alito People of the American Way fire off a broadside against Judge Alito's ruling in *ACLU v. Schundler*, 168 F.3d 92 (3d Cir. 1999). In that case, Judge Alito held that a city was permitted to erect a holiday display that included traditional representations of Christmas along with secular figures and symbols of other religions. The city's holiday display included "not only a crèche, a menorah, and Christmas tree, but also large plastic figures of Santa Claus and Frosty the Snowman, a red sled, and Kwanzaa symbols." According to Judge Alito, the Constitution did not require the religious symbols to be excluded from this eclectic display. Instead, the city was allowed to display religious representations on the same terms that it displayed other types of symbols.

Judge Alito's ruling was a straightforward application of the Supreme Court's holding in *Lynch v. Donnelly*, 465 U.S. 668 (1984), which upheld a virtually identical holiday display. There, a city was allowed to display "a Santa Claus house, reindeer pulling Santa's sleigh, candy-striped poles, a Christmas tree, carolers, cutout figures representing such characters as a clown, an elephant, and a teddy bear, hundreds of colored lights, a large banner that reads 'SEASONS GREETINGS,' and [a] crèche." Indeed, the display in *Schundler* was even more diverse and inclusive than the one approved in *Lynch*.

That *Schundler* was a simple application of settled precedent may explain why the ruling drew support from judges across the political spectrum. Judge Alito's opinion was joined by Judge Marjorie Rendell – an appointee of President Clinton and the wife of Ed Rendell, the former chairman of the Democratic National Committee and current Democratic Governor of Pennsylvania.

The Left's effort to cast aspersions on *Fraise v. Terhune*, 283 F.3d 506 (3d Cir. 2002), fares no better. In that case, Judge Alito upheld the decision of New Jersey prison officials to classify inmates who were members of the Five Percent Nation, or "FPN," as security threats. FPN is a notoriously violent group. It has ties to John Allen Muhammad and John Lee Malvo, the "Beltway Snipers" who murdered a number of innocent people in the Washington, D.C. area. FPN members attacked Hispanic inmates in New York prisons so viciously that the Hispanic inmates formed their own gang, the Latin Kings, to protect themselves. The FPN is the largest group in New Jersey's state prison system and since 1990 had a documented history of not only planning violent attacks in prison, but also using FPN literature to carry coded messages to execute those attacks. Numerous courts have noted FPN's violence, including state and federal courts in New Jersey, New York, and Pennsylvania, as well as the U.S. Court of Appeals for the Fourth Circuit. No wonder, according to the record before the court in *Fraise*, "[m]any in the law enforcement community consider the Five Percent Nation to be 'one of the greatest threats to the social fabric' of the prisons." In addition to the FPN, other groups designated as security threats include violent gangs such as the Aryan Brotherhood, the Latin Kings, Neta, and the Prison Bikers Brotherhood.

Judge Alito's opinion demonstrates that it was because of this history of violence – not because of any religious views – that PFN prisoners were designated as security threats. In so ruling, Judge Alito faithfully applied governing Supreme Court caselaw indicating that prison officials must be shown great deference in managing their violent and unpredictable inmate populations. According to the High Court, running a prison is "peculiarly within the province of the legislative and executive branches of government," and "separation of powers concerns counsel a policy of judicial restraint." *Turner v. Safley*, 482 U.S. 78 (1987). Moreover, New Jersey's policy allowed FPN members to practice their religious beliefs generally, although certain risky practices were not permitted. This is nothing more than a straightforward application of prior Third Circuit precedent, which instructs that, in prison free-exercise cases, the question is whether the inmate has "alternative means of practicing his or her religion generally, not whether [the] inmate has alternative means of engaging in [any] particular practice." *DeHart v. Horn*, 227 F.3d 47, 55 (3d Cir. 2000). Far from betraying any indifference to the rights of religious expression – a dubious proposition in light of the strong record recounted above – *Fraise* actually demonstrates Judge Alito's dedication to stare decisis and the importance of adhering to settled precedent.

Protecting Freedom of Speech

On free speech the far left sounds the alarm because Judge "Alito's opinions suggest that he believes that student speech about morality and 'sin' should not be restricted even when it may offend others." But protecting the right to speech even when others may disagree or be offended is *precisely* what the First Amendment is all about. Even a cursory review of Judge Alito's opinions on the First Amendment shows that they are thoughtful, scholarly, and reasonable.

In *Saxe v. State College Area School District*, 240 F.3d 200 (3d Cir. 2001), writing for a *unanimous* panel that included Judge Rendell –

the wife of Pennsylvania's Democratic Governor Ed Rendell, the former head of the DNC – Judge Alito struck down a school policy that prohibited students from expressing their religious beliefs on the morality of homosexual conduct. In other words, the policy permitted the expression of viewpoints that supported homosexual conduct, but not those that opposed it. Such viewpoint discrimination is *exactly* what the First Amendment prohibits. No wonder the opinion was lauded by the *Pittsburgh Post-Gazette*, which no one would mistake for a hotbed of conservatism. And no wonder the opinion is viewed with suspicion by liberal special interest groups, which wants the courts to support its ultra-liberal agenda, including gay marriage, late-term abortion-on-demand, and the banning of religious viewpoints from public debate.

In *Rappa v. New Castle County*, 18 F.3d 1043 (3d Cir. 1994), Judge Alito joined the opinion of universally respected jurist Judge Becker, to hold that a state law restricting political speech was unconstitutional. Political speech is at the heart of the First Amendment's protections – precisely what the Founders were most concerned about. PFAW's complaint is not with the decision, but with what it dubs the "unorthodox move" of fashioning a test to determine what restrictions the state could place on roadside political campaign signs in the absence of binding Supreme Court precedent. PFAW takes issue with the fact that Judge Becker's opinion did not follow a decision of four justices on the Supreme Court. But four is not a majority. Indeed, the Supreme Court itself has precedent on when a plurality opinion is controlling and when it is not. *See Marks v. United States*, 430 U.S. 188 (1977); *Nichols v. United States*, 511 U.S. 738, 745-46 (1994). Judge Becker was not alone in concluding that there was no binding Supreme Court precedent to apply. The Sixth Circuit unanimously reached the same conclusion in *Discovery Network, Inc. v. City of Cincinnati*, 946 F.2d 464, 470 n.9 (6th Cir. 1991), as did the Eleventh Circuit just recently in *Solantic, LLC v. City of Neptune Beach*, 410

F.3d 1250, 1261 n.10 (11th Cir. 2005). PFAW is once again desperately crying wolf.

In *Sanguigni v. Pittsburgh Board of Public Education*, 968 F.2d 393 (3d Cir. 1992), writing for a unanimous panel of the Third Circuit, Judge Alito considered whether an employee could be terminated for "statements . . . intended to gather opposition to the school administration." Applying binding Supreme Court precedent, it concluded that the employee's termination was consistent with the First Amendment. No other court of appeals or the Supreme Court has ever questioned Judge Alito's scholarly and detailed opinion.

And in *Banks v. Beard*, 399 F.3d 134 (3d Cir. 2005), *certiorari granted:* 2005 U.S. LEXIS 8383 (U.S. Nov. 14, 2005) Judge Alito dissented from an opinion that found prison inmates had a First Amendment right to newspapers and magazines in their cells. Only the far Left could think prisoners were entitled to newspapers and trashy magazines. Felons lose rights when they are convicted – that's why they are prisoners. In his thoughtful dissent, Judge Alito patiently explained that the majority had misapplied the Supreme Court's decision in *Turner v. Safley*, 482 U.S. 78 (1987), a standard that instructs courts to extend considerable deference to judgments of correctional officials. The majority overturned the judgment of the duly elected officials of Pennsylvania – not exactly a "red" state – and imposed their own judgment about how best to run the prison. Judge Alito thus rightly dissented.

Judge Alito's record on the First Amendment and the protection of freedom of speech is simply impeccable. Any suggestion to the contrary is, well, out of the mainstream.

Faithfully Applying the Law to Prisoner Litigation

Judge Alito in a number of cases has safeguarded the rights of prisoners – particularly inmates who claim that their convictions were tainted by racial discrimination. For example, in *Brinson v. Vaughn*,

398 F.3d 225 (3d Cir. 2005), Judge Alito reversed the district court's dismissal of an African-American inmate's habeas corpus petition; the inmate was challenging the state prosecutor's decision to strike a number of African-Americans from the jury. Judge Alito ruled that the inmate had made out a prima facie case of a constitutional violation and that, although the inmate's petition was filed late, it was proper to toll the statute of limitations. Similarly, in *Williams v. Price*, 343 F.3d 223 (3d Cir. 2003), Judge Alito granted a writ of habeas corpus to an African-American inmate after a witness stated that a juror had uttered derogatory remarks about African-Americans during an encounter in the courthouse following the trial.

Nothing about Judge Alito's ruling in *Poole v. Family Court of New Castle County*, 368 F.3d 263 (3d Cir. 2004), decided unanimously by a bipartisan panel, reasonably can be read as evincing a lack of sympathy to prisoner litigants. That case presented an arcane question involving the Federal Rules of Civil Procedure – the sort of issue only a lawyer could love.

The *Poole* case arose when an inmate sued numerous parties, including prison officials, claiming that they were limiting his access to a minor he represented to be his son. The district court dismissed all of Poole's claims, in part because it found them to be frivolous. However, Poole did not immediately receive notice that his lawsuit was dismissed. He was being transferred to a different prison at the time and the district court clerk, who did not know about the transfer, sent the notice to the original prison address. After receiving notice, the prisoner sought to appeal.

Writing for a unanimous Third Circuit panel, Judge Alito held that the prisoner had not filed his appeal within the time allotted by the rules. This outcome flowed inexorably from the text of Federal Rule of Civil Procedure 77(d), which instructs that "[l]ack of notice of the entry by the clerk does not affect the time to appeal or relieve or authorize the court to relieve or authorize the court to relieve a party for failure to appeal within the time allowed," and Federal Rule of Appellate Procedure 4(a)(6), which required Poole to move to reopen the time to file an appeal within seven days of receiving notice. As sympathetic as Judge Alito and his colleagues might have been to the prisoner's situation, the court was bound by the rules, and could not have reached any other result without ignoring the governing law. Judge Alito's opinion thus stands as a further testament to his commitment to faithfully applying statutory text, no matter how personally distasteful he may find the outcome.

It cannot be overemphasized that the *Poole* case was decided unanimously, by a bipartisan panel of judges. One of the judges who joined Judge Alito was appointed by President Carter, and the other judge had served as Acting Solicitor General in the Carter Administration. With that in mind it is hard to see how this case could possibly be an example of Judge Alito being "outside of the mainstream."

Criticisms of Judge Alito's decision in *Rompilla v. Horn*, 355 F.3d 233 (3d Cir. 2004), seem to come from the fact that there are those who overlook the fact that some cases present hard questions, and that judges operating in good faith can come to different conclusions about what the law requires. In *Rompilla*, a convicted murderer filed suit alleging that he had been convicted because his lawyer had not adequately represented him. The prisoner's trial attorneys decided not to search his school, medical, court and prison records for any mitigating factors that would counsel against imposing the death penalty. Instead, they believed that the best way to find such evidence was to interview several family members and health experts. None of these witnesses mentioned the prisoner's childhood neglect, mental problems, or any other facts that might have helped his case.

It is crucial to a fair-minded understanding of the matter to recognize that ineffective assistance of counsel cases are, by their very nature, extremely fact intensive. In fact, after Judge Alito in a 2-1 opinion held against the prisoner, the full Third Circuit by a 6-5 vote decided not to rehear the case – thereby effectively affirming Judge Alito's ruling. Even the district court, which ruled in favor of the prisoner, acknowledged that it was a close call "because trial counsel performed so admirably according to my review of the record. . . . [T]rial counsel were intelligent, diligent, and devoted to their task of representing [Rompilla]." The fact that the *en banc* Third Circuit agreed with his analysis in a 6-5 vote and the Supreme Court disagreed in a 5-4 vote indicates that the district court got it right in describing the case as "a close call."

Nor was the Third Circuit the only court to follow the course charted in *Rompilla*. Rather, Judge Alito's ruling that the prisoner's trial representation was not so deficient as to offend the Sixth Amendment was consistent with rulings from a number of other circuits. One court held that "the test for ineffectiveness is not whether counsel could have done more; perfection is not required. Nor is the test whether the best criminal defense attorneys might have done more. Instead the test is . . . whether what [counsel] did was within the 'wide range of reasonable professional assistance.'" *Waters v. Thomas*, 46 F.3d 1506, 1518 (11th Cir. 1995) (en banc) (quoting *Strickland v. Washington*, 466 U.S. 668, 689 (1984)). Another held that a defendant is not entitled "to the best available counsel or the most prudent strategies"; instead, the Sixth Amendment is "satisfied when the lawyer chooses a professionally competent strategy that secures for the accused the benefit of an adversarial trial." *Kokoralies v. Gilmore*, 131 F.3d 692, 696 (7th Cir. 1997).

Finally, some of the Left, such as PFAW, have criticized Judge Alito over his decision in *Pemberthy v. Beyer*, 19 F.3d 857 (3d Cir. 1994), in which a unanimous Third Circuit panel upheld on habeas corpus review a state court conviction for drug offenses and theft. Writing for the court, Judge Alito rejected the convict's argument that it was unconstitutional for the prosecutor to dismiss five Spanish-speaking jurors because the translation of taped conversations in Spanish was expected to be hotly contested at trial. His critics neglect to mention that the outcome was dictated both by the deferential standard of review required by Congress in habeas cases, as well as by the Supreme Court's own precedent in *Hernandez v. New York*, 500 U.S. 352 (1991). Moreover, the Ninth Circuit – hardly known as a bastion of conservatism – later followed the same reasoning regarding bilingual jurors, noting that "[w]hen, as here, a district court is faced with a jury that includes one or more bilingual jurors and the taped conversations are in a language other than English, restrictions on the jurors who are conversant with the foreign tongue is not only appropriate, it [sic] may in fact be essential. . . . The rules of evidence and the expert testimony would prove of little use if a self-styled expert in the deliberations were free to give his or her opinion on this crucial issue, unknown to the parties." *United States v. Fuentes-Montijo*, 68 F.3d 352, 355 (9th Cir. 1995).

Faithful Enforcement of Immigration Laws

Judge Alito's numerous immigration decisions defy classification as either "liberal" or "conservative," but instead reflect his usual commitment to applying the law to the case at hand impartially. For example, in *Fatin v. INS*, 12 F.3d 1233 (3d Cir. 1998), which is also discussed above, Judge Alito gave the term "refugee" in the Immigration and Nationality Act a broad reading. The petitioner in that case, a female citizen of Iran who fled the country just before the fall of the Shah and entered the United States as a nonimmigrant student, sought asylum because "she would be persecuted in Iran simply because she is a woman." Judge Alito held that she was eligible for asylum if she could show that compliance with Iran's "gender specific laws and repressive social norms" (such as the requirement that women wear veils in public) would be deeply abhorrent to her.

Judge Alito has recognized that asylum cases are "among the most difficult" confronting the federal courts, and that "[m]uch is obviously at stake" in those cases. Part of the difficulty, as scholars have noted, is that "[a]sylum determinations often depend critically on a determination of the credibility of the applicant, for she will usually be the only available witness to the critical adjudicative facts of the case."[8] Congress requires federal judges to defer to the credibility assessments of Immigration Judges (IJs) who hear testimony in the first instance, "unless any reasonable adjudicator would be compelled to conclude to the contrary." 8 U.S.C. § 1252(b)(4)(B). As Judge Alito has noted, the highly deferential standard Congress has chosen "puts us in the uncomfortable position of deferring to a credibility determination about which we are skeptical. But the statute leaves us no alternative."

Still, Judge Alito has been willing to reject an IJ's credibility determination in appropriate cases. In *Gui Cun Liu v. Ashcroft*, 372 F.3d 529 (3d Cir. 2004), the IJ improperly rejected a married couple's documentary evidence of the forced abortions the wife had suffered in China, even though the abortion certificates corroborated their account of the persecution they had suffered. The IJ had given no weight to the abortion certificates because they had not been authenticated in accordance with regulations, even though the couple had attempted to authenticate them and had been told by the Chinese government that it was impossible to do so. Judge Alito held that they "should have been allowed to attempt to prove the authenticity of the abortion certificates through other means, especially where (as here) attempts to abide by the requirements of [the regulations] failed due to lack of cooperation from government officials in the country of alleged persecution." Because the corroborating evidence should have been considered, Judge Alito rejected the IJ's finding that the couple was not credible.

But that is not good enough for left-wing groups like PFAW, who seem to think that any illegal alien seeking asylum in the United States should be granted it. In their report on Judge Alito group complains about Judge Alito's dissent in *Dia v. Ashcroft*, 353 F.3d 228 (3d Cir.

2003) (en banc). In that case, an IJ had found an illegal alien's testimony incredible, in part because of substantial inconsistencies in his testimony and its general implausibility in certain particulars. Despite the statutory standard – which requires deference to the IJ "unless *any reasonable adjudicator* would be *compelled* to conclude to the contrary" – the majority rejected the IJ's findings simply because it was *possible* for one to reach a different conclusion. In effect, the majority stood the congressional standard on its head. Judge Alito – joined by one appointee of President Carter and another Republican appointee – dissented on the ground that the court was compelled by statute to defer to the IJ. Judge Alito noted that he might not have made the same credibility determinations as the IJ, but his responsibility was to apply the "reasonable adjudicator" standard that Congress had enacted.

Judge Alito dissented in *Chang v. INS*, 119 F.3d 1055 (1993), for similar reasons. In that case, a Chinese engineer who led a delegation to the United States violated the Chinese Security Law because he did not report his suspicions that some of his colleagues were planning to defect; the engineer then remained in the United States and sought asylum because he feared prosecution for his legal violations. The IJ denied his request for asylum because the prosecution he might have faced in China was not politically motivated; in fact, the engineer never expressed any political disagreement with the Chinese government. Under the law as enacted by Congress, the IJ's determination was entitled to deference unless no reasonable fact finder could have reached the same conclusion. Although the panel majority refused to defer to the IJ's fact finding, Judge Alito followed the congressional directive and would have deferred, because the IJ's decision was at least reasonable in the absence of any testimony that the engineer was politically opposed to the government of China.

Judge Alito has also been criticized for his dissent in *Lee v. Ashcroft*, 368 F.3d 218 (3d Cir. 2004). The issue in that case was whether a conviction for filing a false tax return was an aggravated felony that made resident aliens subject to removal from the country. To Judge Alito, it was a straightforward matter of statutory interpretation: An aggravated felony was generally defined by Congress as an offense that "involves fraud or deceit in which the loss to the victim or victims exceeds $10,000." Because the offense at issue – filing a false tax return – involved fraud or deceit, he concluded that it met the statutory definition of an aggravated felony.

Judge Alito does not reflexively conclude, however, that any felony is the sort of offense that makes an alien subject to removal. For example, in *Oyebanji v. Gonzalez*, 418 F.3d 260 (3d Cir. 2005), a resident alien had been ordered removed for committing a "crime of violence" after he was convicted of vehicular homicide. The Supreme Court had already decided in *Leocal v. Ashcroft*, 543 U.S. 1 (2004) that crimes involving only a showing of negligence did not qualify as "crimes of violence," but the Supreme Court specifically left open the question of whether crimes requiring only a showing of recklessness were "crimes of violence." Judge Alito held that they were not, thereby sparing the alien from removal under the immigration laws.

The Vanguard Recusal: An Absolute Non-Issue

Unfortunately for the left-wing special interests groups, their gross misrepresentations of Judge Alito's record have failed to make any headway with the public. It was clear from the very beginning of this process that Judge Alito is one of the most experienced and qualified persons ever to be nominated to the Supreme Court. With recent polls showing that the American people support Judge Alito's confirmation by a 2-1 majority[9], the Left is now scraping the bottom of the barrel in an attempt to smear Judge Alito. Specifically, they have attempted to raise a conflict of interest issue concerning recusal in a case involving Vanguard Funds, which held some of Judge Alito's assets. *See Monga v. Ottenberg*, 43 Fed. Appx. 523 (2002). A brief review of the facts of the case and a clear reading of the federal ethics statutes, however, reveals that Judge Alito violated none of his ethical responsibilities.

In the case at issue, a bankrupt plaintiff accused Vanguard of improperly disbursing the proceeds of her account, which, pursuant to a Massachusetts court order, Vanguard made available to the plaintiff's creditors. Therefore, Vanguard had no direct interest in the case and was only a third party that was holding the funds either for the bankrupt plaintiff or her creditors By the time the case reached the Third Circuit, the case was not even about the Vanguard disbursement itself. Rather, it was about the effect of the court order.

In the opinion of three independent legal experts[10] Judge Alito's initial participation in the appeal was not improper under 26 U.S.C. §455, the federal ethics statute which established the governing rules. Judge Alito did not own stock in Vanguard. Instead, he was a fund investor and, therefore, more like a depositor in a bank with no ownership interest or control over disbursements. Moreover, according to one expert, even if he had owned stock, "the amount involved in the plaintiff's dispute with Vanguard was not enough in my opinion to create an 'appearance of impropriety.'" Finally, Vanguard had no financial stake in the dispute and therefore could not be harmed or benefited by the outcome of the case. Either way, Vanguard was going to distribute the money to one of the parties.

When he first ascended to the Third Circuit Court of Appeals Judge Alito properly listed Vanguard funds among his assets, but the court's computer program, which was supposed to automatically keep judges from sitting on cases involving parties they have listed, had a glitch. It was this program which randomly, but mistakenly, assigned the case to Judge Alito and two other judges.

The outcome of the case was clear whether Judge Alito participated or not. When the case was initially reviewed by the Third Circuit, Judge Alito was part of a unanimous three-judge panel affirming the district court's decision. After a complaint by the plaintiff made Judge Alito aware of the possible conflict, he immediately informed Third Circuit Chief Judge Edward Roy Becker, so that a new panel could review the decision. He did this despite the fact that he was not required to do so by the canons of judicial ethics. The second panel, like the first, unanimously rejected the plaintiff's claims. Clearly, the plaintiff's complaint against Judge Alito was little more than an attempt to keep alive a lawsuit that had no merit.

[1] See People for the American Way, The Record of Samuel Alito: A Preliminary Review (Oct. 31, 2005) ("PFAW Report").

[2] Warren Richey, *On Abortion, a Nuanced Stand*, CHRISTIAN SCIENCE MONITOR, Nov. 2, 2005.

[3] Jonathan H. Adler, *A Brilliant Judicial Mind*, WALL ST. J., Nov. 1, 2005.

[4] Karlyn Bowman, *What the Public Thinks About One Key Issue in Alito's Nomination*, ROLL CALL, Nov. 2, 2005.

[5] Ruth Bader Ginsburg and Brenda Feigen Fasteau, "The Legal Status of Women under Federal Law," Columbia Law School Equal Rights Advocacy Project (1974)(available at: http://www.eppc.org/publications/pubID.2363/pub_detail.asp)

[6] Laurence Tribe, Professor of Law at Harvard who represented Al Gore in 2000 said, "One of the most curious things about *Roe* is that, behind its own verbal smokescreen, the substantive judgment on which it rests is nowhere to be found." *The Supreme Court, 1972 Term—Foreword: Toward a Model of Roles in the Due Process of Life and Law*, 87 Harvard Law Review 1, 7 (1973). Cass Sunstein, Professor of Law at the University of Chicago and a Democratic adviser on judicial nominations has made some interesting comments about the *Roe's* status as "super-duper precedent" when he admitted, "What I think is that it just doesn't have the stable status of *Brown* or *Miranda* because it's been under internal and external assault pretty much from the beginning.... As a constitutional matter, I think *Roe* was way overreached." Quoted in: Brian McGuire, *Roe v. Wade an Issue Ahead of Alito Hearing*, New York Sun November 15, 2005. Alan Dershowitz, Professor of Law at Harvard, has likened *Roe* to the *Bush v. Gore* decision, which he has fiercely criticized. *Supreme Injustice: How the High Court Hijacked Election 2000* (New York: Oxford) 2001, p. 194.

[7] Ruth Bader Ginsburg, *Essay: Some Thoughts on Autonomy and Equality in Relation to Roe v. Wade*, 63 N.C.L. 375, 385 (1985).

[8] David A. Martin, *Reforming Asylum Adjudication: On Navigating the Coast of Bohemia*, 138 U. PA. L. REV. 1247, 1281-82 (1990) (footnotes omitted).

[9] Lydia Saad, *Americans Generally Favor Alito Appointment: Closer to Roberts than to Miers in popularity*, The Gallup Poll (November 14, 2005)

[10] Geoffrey C. Hazard, Jr., Trustee Professor of Law, University of Pennsylvania; Thomas D. Morgan, Oppenheim Professor of Antitrust & Trade Regulation Law, George Washington University School of Law; Ronald D. Rotunda, Professor of Law, George Mason University School of Law